Goldwin + Katie Beisel

LIFEKEYS

LifeKeys Resources

LifeKeys
LifeKeys Discovery Workbook
LifeKeys Leadership Resource
Find Your Fit: LifeKeys for Teens
Find Your Fit Discovery Workbook
Find Your Fit Leader's Guide
LifeDirections
SoulTypes
Work It Out

For more information: www.lifekeys.com

LifeKeys

DISCOVERING...
WHO YOU ARE • WHY YOU'RE HERE • WHAT YOU DO BEST

JANE A.G. KISE
DAVID STARK
SANDRA KREBS HIRSH

BETHANY HOUSE PUBLISHERS
MINNEAPOLIS, MINNESOTA 55438

Published by Bethany House Publishers
A Ministry of Bethany Fellowship, Inc.
11400 Hampshire Avenue South
Minneapolis, Minnesota 55438
www.bethanyhouse.com

Printed in the United States of America by
Bethany Press International, Minneapolis, Minnesota 55438

Library of Congress Cataloging-in-Publication Data

Kise, Jane A. G.
   Lifekeys : discovering who you are, why you're here, and what you do best /
Jane A.G. Kise, David Stark, Sandra Krebs Hirsh.
      p. cm.
   Includes bibliographical references (p.).
ISBN 1–55661–871–9
   1. Success—Religious aspects—Christianity. 2. Self-actualization
(Psychology)—Religious aspects—Christianity. 3. Gifts, Spiritual. 4. Lay
ministry. I. Stark, David, 1955–   . II. Hirsh, Sandra Krebs. III. Title.
BV4598.3.K57   1996
248.4—dc20   96–25278
                                                    CIP

To the people of Christ Presbyterian Church,
especially those who have participated in our classes
and enriched these pages through their insights,
experiences, and suggestions.

JANE A. G. KISE is a freelance writer and management consultant in the fields of strategic planning and team building. She holds a B.A. from Hamline University and an M.B.A. in finance from the University of Minnesota. She is the coauthor of a book on personality types at work.

DAVID STARK is a pastor at Christ Presbyterian Church in Edina, Minnesota, and founder and director of training for Church Innovations. His small-group materials, *People Together*, are widely used in churches in a variety of denominations. He holds an M.Div. from Princeton Theological Seminary and has led dozens of workshops and seminars throughout the United States.

SANDRA KREBS HIRSH is a management consultant, providing career management and organizational development consultation. She holds graduate degrees in American Studies and Industrial Relations. One of her books on the Myers-Briggs Type Indicator® has sold over a million copies. She is much in demand worldwide for her expertise in Human Resources and Organizational Development.

ACKNOWLEDGMENTS

This project grew out of the efforts of a whole team of people. We would especially like to thank:

Richard N. Bolles, for reading the manuscript and providing us with key suggestions.

Judy Gentry, for her partnership with us in the early stages of developing these materials.

Charette Barta, for her encouragement in shepherding *LifeKeys* toward publication.

Rev. Judie Ritchie, for her help with spiritual direction for each personality type.

Dorothy Cummings, Tom and Terri Gulliford, Vicki Manuel, and Laurel Schnabel—members of the original team at church.

And all of the people whose stories are told anonymously in these pages, for their willingness to enrich this book with their lives.

CONTENTS

PREFACE

Have you discovered the keys to a fulfilling life?
Do the roles you play or the work you do fit with who you are?
Does the life you lead give you a sense of purpose and meaning?

For a staggering number of people—even those who appear to have their act together—the answer to these questions is "NO!"

This book grew out of our efforts to help members of our congregation identify *LifeKeys*—truths about who they are, why they are here, and what they do best that will add significance and direction to their lives. All around us people were saying:

"I'm curious about this notion of having a purpose in life. Is there anything to it?"

"There are more layoffs coming—I wonder if I should rethink my career goals."

"I feel pulled in another direction. Should I take a fresh look at my options?"

"I don't seem to fit in anywhere or have talents anyone wants."

We—Jane, David, and Sandra—believe that the best answers to these questions are spiritual answers. *LifeKeys* is our process for helping these friends—and you—find those answers. We'd like to tell you how it all began. . . .

David: Being someone who tends toward large-scale dreams, I wanted to see the Church become a place where people could discover their potential and by God's grace develop it in significant ways. In my early ministry experiences, I saw a change in people when they understood their gifts and their passions—in short, when they found their *LifeKeys*. They were confidently able to step out in faith where they believed God was leading them. If we concentrate too much on our weaknesses, as all too often the Church has done, we miss discovering the God-given capabilities that outfit us for the missions God had in mind when each one of us was uniquely created.

Through a series of serendipitous events, I was asked to teach a seminar on gift identification for the women's association at our church. While I used an existing curriculum, I soon realized that the approach missed the emphasis I wanted. There wasn't enough information about the merits of each person's gifts; people needed more material to process what they learned about themselves; and they weren't convinced that God loved them enough to gift them. Even in our "healthy" church, people needed more.

I realized that creating a better approach was a bigger task than I wanted to tackle on my own. I needed a team of writers, organizers, and others with a heart for helping people discover what God could do through them.

Jane: I participated in that early women's class David taught. Sitting in the seminar, I realized for the first time how unique my upbringing was. Coming from a family where my four brothers and I were encouraged to find out how and where we could be of service, the class confirmed much of what I already believed God had in mind for my mission. However, most of the other women at my table were disheartened. They felt dwarfed by the suggested standards of spirituality and giftedness. Somehow they lacked the foundational belief that out of a heart of love God had chosen the best for them, so they were disappointed in what they discovered about themselves. I heard comments such as, "I don't like my gifts," "I want to be someone else," "I'm not really valuable to God."

When David asked for help with creating a richer process on the same subject matter, I spontaneously put down my name. I was sure that this concept of finding *LifeKeys*, done correctly, could help people experience what my family had given me. I also knew that David needed an organizer—he readily admits to being a visionary, not an administrator! I could put his thoughts on paper and think through class arrangements.

As the project grew, so did my role, especially as we realized that people needed a notebook that included the teachings as well as their self-discovery exercises. Three years later, I constantly hear from people—at church, on the phone, even at the supermarket—about the positive choices they have made as a result of understanding their own *LifeKeys*. It's amazing what happens when God puts a team together!

Sandra: While I had been active in church throughout most of my life, I had also been deeply hurt by the actions of some religious people who had made me feel like the "unwashed among the washed." I became a soloist in my spiritual journey, helping others through my career in human resources consulting but avoiding formal religious ties. However, close to the time I met David and Jane, my soul was longing for a more meaningful role. I again wanted to make the church a part of my life.

On a dreary November day while trying to find some papers, I looked out my office window and noticed a man dashing across the parking lot. He was obviously trying to get somewhere in a hurry. A few minutes later as I prepared to leave, the same man was standing outside my office door!

"Are you Sandra Hirsh—who works with personality types?" he said breathlessly.

"Yes, and who are you?" I asked.

"I'm David Stark, a pastor at Christ Presbyterian Church," he stated, and went on to add more about *my* home church! He explained the course he wanted to develop and asked, "Would you be interested in advising me on this part?"

I said, "I'd be glad to hear what you teach. I'll let you know if I can add anything of value." David claims that I later said he required a *great deal* of my help, but in truth I was impressed with his vision and eagerly joined the team.

This chance(?) encounter led to what my soul was seeking—a community of faith (in *my own* church at that) and a chance to serve with others in a meaningful way that matched my gifts.

Through a lot of trial and error, prayer, and the contributions of dozens of people, we began to formulate first a class, then a notebook, and finally *LifeKeys* as you now see it. For us, the greatest joy is seeing the powerful impact this God-centered self-discovery process has on people. The three themes that play over and over again in our materials are:

- God created you and therefore values you highly.
- God created you uniquely, and there is genuinely only one of you.

• God, from the foundation of the world, had good works in mind for you to do.

Hearing these themes releases people—ourselves included—in ways that we have seldom seen. We hope that as you work your way through this book, the uniqueness and value of your own life will begin to surface. Somewhere, deep inside of you, are *LifeKeys* awaiting your discovery. Join us as we explore how your giftedness, personality, values, and purpose provide the keys to a meaningful life. When you understand how you have been created, God's Spirit can honestly do far more through you than you could ask or even imagine.

LifeKey 1

God has an important part for you— yes, YOU—to play!

CHAPTER 1

LifeKeys to Who You Are, Why You're Here, and What You Do Best

> *I had been my whole life a bell, and never knew it until at that moment I was lifted and struck.*[1]
>
> —Annie Dillard

The school orchestra: that safe haven for a positive first experience with music. Even if you were tone-deaf and had trouble catching the beat, the director could still find a place for you. She might suggest another instrument: "Lisa, with your strong lungs, I think the trombone might be a better fit for you than the flute." Or, with encouragement, she'd build on your strengths: "Bill, you have the best sense of rhythm in the string section, but we're short of drummers—would you consider switching?"

When the director created this atmosphere, orchestra was great. It was a chance to get out of class, make as much noise as you wanted, and not have to worry about mistakes. What could be more fun? After all, there were 29 flutes, 18 clarinets, a host of cornets and saxophones—so many players that it was impossible to guess the source of any bad notes.

In this inclusive atmosphere, students could keep trying until they found an instrument that made them feel a part of the orchestra. Some stayed in the third row of clarinets all the way through high school, supplying the low harmony that allowed the melody to shine. Some switched to unusual instruments—oboe or

---

[1] Annie Dillard, *Pilgrim at Tinker Creek* (New York: Harper & Row, 1974), p. 35.

baritone saxophone—balancing the sound of the group. Others played as well as they could, but more than anything contributed a fun-loving spirit. And in some way, everyone went on to be a star. Besides the drummer who now plays with a major symphony, one band produced:

- A pianist who uses her musical skills as an occupational therapist;
- Two trumpet players who pass on their love of music by conducting high school bands;
- A trombonist who found a career in sound-mixing;
- A flute player who put her talents to use on mission outreach trips;
- And many more who never played another note, yet who gained from their orchestra experience a sense of the richness that music bestows on life.

Whatever their path, young musicians who played under such an encouraging director enjoyed the experience of being a part of something bigger than themselves, of learning to harmonize with and benefit from the efforts of others.

This book attempts to create that same safe atmosphere for *you*—a place where you can discover *LifeKeys* that will help you orchestrate your life and find a path that leads to a sense of purpose or individual calling.

Think about how Webster's defines "orchestrate." It means "to arrange or combine so as to achieve a maximum effect." "Orchestration" means "harmonious organization."[2] Wouldn't it be nice to know that your life is harmoniously organized—not just *when* you do things, but *how, where,* and *why* as well? Wouldn't it be refreshing to feel that you have put together all the pieces of *you* in a meaningful way?

But life isn't as safe as a school orchestra, is it?

Perhaps you are one of the lucky ones who have found a good fit in life, settling somehow into a good place. You feel effective. You find meaning in your activities. If that describes you, we hope that *LifeKeys* will provide a structured method to help you continue to make choices that lead to fulfillment.

---

[2] *Webster's New Collegiate Dictionary* (Springfield, Mass.: G. & C. Merriam Company, 1977), p. 807.

Many more people, however, struggle to find *any* place where they feel as though they fit. You may never have had a chance to explore what kind of "instrument" you might play. Maybe your life was orchestrated for you long ago by a parent or someone else who was sure they knew what suited you best. It was as if they purchased a pricey, nonreturnable instrument for you, leaving you no choice about what you would play in life. Or perhaps your orchestration was somewhat haphazard—you are where you are more by accident than by design.

Perhaps your parents thought your special interests were a waste of time. Or teachers or counselors discouraged you from trying anything new. Or you felt left out, as if you were destined for the mundane, the drudgery of run-of-the-mill duty for the rest of your days.

There *is* a place for you in the orchestra of life. This book and the thoughts that fill it came about because countless other people are asking the same questions you are: *Where is my part? What is my contribution? How can I give of myself in a way that gives meaning to me and goodness to others?* Each *LifeKey* we will explore together adds to your understanding of who you are, why you're here, and what you do best. When you are able to view your various *LifeKeys* as a whole, you can begin to orchestrate a fulfilling life—not merely for personal ends, but to bring harmony to you *and* your world as you live all that God has built into you.

In *What Color Is Your Parachute?*, a book that was personally helpful to each of us, Richard N. Bolles probably best describes the concept of your unique mission in life.

a) To exercise that Talent which you particularly came to Earth to use—your greatest gift which you most delight to use

b) in the place(s) or setting(s) which God has caused to appeal to you the most

c) and for those purposes which God most needs to have done in the world.[3]

LifeKeys guides you through the process of finding that unique

---

[3]Richard N. Bolles, *What Color Is Your Parachute?* (Berkeley, Calif.: Ten Speed Press, 1996), p. 449. Copyright © 1996 by Richard N. Bolles. Used with permission.

mission God had in mind when He created you. We first help you to find your greatest gift—as Bolles describes in *a*) above—in the chapters on life gifts and spiritual gifts. Next, the chapters on personality types and passions help you to recognize the places or settings which God has caused to appeal to you the most, as Bolles describes in *b*). Finally, the chapters on values and life choices can aid your process of discovering the purposes for which God most needs your help, as described in *c*).

As you read, keep in mind that you are searching for your personal *LifeKeys*—the gifts that *you* take delight in using and the places that appeal to *you* the most, in accordance with how God has uniquely designed *you*. Examining yourself from this God-centered perspective readies you for those purposes God needs to have done. Without such an exploration, you may miss a life that harmonizes with God's plan for you.

What Keeps Us From Discovering Our *LifeKeys*?

As we used these materials at our church, we found that the majority of the participants in our classes—and these were people from *all* walks of life—struggled with our underlying premise: that they were gifted by God! Their doubts came from diverse sources. Some had been tossed from their current track by a downsizing company or changing industry needs. Some were approaching the second half of their lives and were feeling a vague lack of purpose. For many, though, the doubts came from deeper sources.

Some assumed that their gifts were insignificant. We heard people say, "My talents are absolutely unimpressive. My only option is to be content to sit and listen or watch, right?" Assuming that only the world-class talents of virtuosos are worthy can be a major stumbling block. Our culture tends to celebrate certain gifts at exceptional levels. If you're not successful in business or government leadership, athletics, acting, or public speaking, it is easy to underrate or shortchange yourself.

However, if you compare yourself to earthly standards, you miss one of the most amazing messages God has for you—you were created in a way that reflects God!

> Then God said, "Let us make humankind in our image, according to our likeness, and let them have dominion over

the fish of the sea, and over the birds of the air, and over the cattle, and over all the wild animals of the earth, and over every creeping thing that creeps upon the earth."

So God created humankind in his own image, in the image of God he created them; male and female he created them. (Genesis 1:26–27, NRSV)

If you view your gifts as insignificant, remember that somewhere inside of you is the *image of God*. If God considers your soul a fitting home, He desires that you think of yourself in that way as well. Your Creator has granted you the necessary resources to reflect His love to the world.

Certainly some gifts are easier to recognize than others. When a three-year-old can sit down at the piano and play by ear a song she heard just once, people notice. When an athlete takes the Olympic gold, people notice. When someone makes millions of dollars before the age of thirty, people notice. Yet even if your gifts are less recognizable, they are indeed as worthy as the gifts to which the world pays attention. Consider the person who has a special knack for encouraging others to try again, or the friend who imparts a gentle, calming influence amidst a crisis, or the young adult who can easily transform chaos into an organized filing system. Given the biases of our society, these individuals may not be recognized as the gifted people they are.

This book is meant to encourage you to take a fresh look at the part you were meant to play. Your part is unique to you—your personality, values, and gifts. You have been given a special place in the orchestra of life. As one little boy put it, "I know I'm worth something, because God don't make no junk." The same holds true for you—you resemble God.

Some assumed that they were missing the "right" gift. Do you mourn along with Dorothy's friends in the land of Oz because you lack "a brain . . . a heart . . . the nerve?" Many are convinced that they are of little value because they don't have the "right" gift. By fixating on that one "right" gift, they often miss noticing the multiple gifts they already have.

This focus can make otherwise talented people feel inadequate. One woman belittled herself, saying, "All I do is cook meals for the sick and pray." In truth, her prayer and visitation ministry was a vital part of her church's spiritual life and a significant help to those in need.

For you created my inmost being; you knit me together in my mother's womb.

I praise you because I am fearfully and wonderfully made; your works are wonderful, I know that full well.

My frame was not hidden from you when I was made in the secret place. When I was woven together in the depths of the earth, your eyes saw my unformed body. All the days ordained for me were written in your book before one of them came to be. (Psalm 139:13–16)

Remember, God gave you everything you need—the truly right gifts chosen just for you. What may be lacking is confidence in *your knowledge* of what God can do through you.

Some people claimed that their gifts don't mesh the way they should. Do you feel like a violinist with drumsticks instead of a bow? If you feel mismatched, what you may need is a different perspective. A swimmer, for example, could not fathom why God had given her an uncanny talent for distance swimming without also giving her the body type she needed in order to be a really great swimmer. She could time each lap of a twenty-lap race perfectly for each segment of the race but wasn't tall enough to beat the competition. Because she loved swimming and the water so much, she was frustrated. Turning to coaching, however, she finally made sense of her natural gifts for stroke mechanics and race strategies, along with her passion for the sport itself.

Others felt as if they had spent their life practicing the wrong instruments. You may wonder how your training matches with who you *now* are. One of the participants in our class, a fifty-two-year-old dentist, said, "An eighteen-year-old who didn't know what he was doing (me!) chose my career." However, your training may some day be used in ways you can't yet imagine. For example, Dr. Paul Brand, a renowned surgeon, could not understand why God had led him to spend four years in architectural engineering school, delaying his entry into medical school. Years later when he worked as a doctor with lepers, though, he realized that God had plans for those engineering skills. His surgical expertise allowed him to pioneer techniques for repairing hands damaged by leprosy. He also designed tools with special features to safeguard the insensitive hands of lepers, allowing them to find useful employment. The tools could only have been designed by someone who understood both engineering principles and the medical needs of those with leprosy. His engineering training was just what God had in mind!

Some wondered why they feel drawn to certain areas, but lack the gifts they believe are required. Consider that within each arena, however, there are many roles to play. For example, one young mother taught Sunday school quite skillfully for five years. Despite her success, she felt completely drained after each class, as if she were teaching out of determination instead of a gift for teaching. After much prayer, she decided to channel her love and passion for children into an administrative role, helping others to teach by providing teacher workshops, organizing classroom supplies, and making other resources available. This new role allowed her to use her gifts and continue to serve out of her passion for children. Gone was the feeling of being drained. Along came a sense of enthusiasm. In her realignment, she influenced not just a single class of children, but every child in the church.

Some doubted that there is any part for them to play. If you can't believe that God has a use for you, humor us for a moment. Perhaps you haven't given yourself the time to discover your *LifeKeys*. Or your life hasn't taken you to settings where you could stumble upon them. If that sounds like you, consider that you might be like a fidgety drummer awaiting your opportunity to shine.

Back in school, kids who wanted to be drummers needed imagination. While other orchestra members got to play real instruments from the start, first-year drummers began their lessons on practice pads—blocks of wood with a rubber circle glued on top.

Pads have two advantages for the director: they're quiet, and students are forced to work on technique, not noisemaking. Pads have two disadvantages for students: they're quiet, and students are forced to work on technique, not noisemaking.

But for the drummers who persisted, the big day finally came when they graduated to the real instruments. They took charge of the snare drum, the cymbals, the marimba, the bass drum, maybe even a whole drum set. Just one drummer could fill the school cafeteria with enough rhythm to shake the windows in the principal's office up above!

The thrill of finally hearing the real thing! Passing those pads to the next group of new drummers, they exulted in the crashes and cadences their nimble sticking now produced. This was music!

No wonder so many drummers went home to their garages and started their own bands.

Now What About You?

If you have never played the instrument God designed for you, a rich experience awaits you. However, before you can receive and enjoy that feeling, you need to discover your niche—the niche that God promises us is there:

> For we are God's workmanship, created in Christ Jesus to do good works, which God prepared in advance for us to do. (Ephesians. 2:10)

But you want a different assignment? You can't read the notes or follow the score? Please believe us—perhaps you haven't yet heard the music. Or your time has not yet come.

Do you see yourself in any of our stories about others who questioned their gifts? Can you only picture yourself as a "swimmer," unable to envision taking your place as a coach or referee or trainer? Or is it difficult to see yourself as a "teacher" able to switch to administration of an educational endeavor? Or do you struggle with understanding how some of your skills or past experiences could possibly mesh with what you can do now?

Of even greater concern, have you given up on yourself? Have you taken whatever comes along? Do you doubt that God has a plan for you—that there is a Creator who truly cares about you and your search for meaning? We and those who have worked through these materials know with certainty that God cares, that there is a connection between who we are and what God has in mind for us. It may take effort to find that connection, but the effort is worth it both for yourself and for others in your life.

And God passionately wants you to find that connection. As Keith Miller and Bruce Larson put it,

> All that we are meant to be! God's dream for each of us is so vastly greater than the largest dream we have for ourselves. But what is his dream for us? I believe he has given us clues to what that dream is. And the longings and yearnings buried in each of us often provide those clues. It is like being on a cosmic treasure hunt. Follow one clue and it will lead you to

another . . . and then to another . . . until you find the treasure himself. For to find God and his ultimate will for us is to find ourselves. This is the discovery for which all of creation stands on tiptoe—to see God's sons and daughters coming into their own.[4]

Join us through the pages of this book and allow yourself to uncover your gifts, personality, values, and passions—your *LifeKeys*—that instrument God meant you to be. Place before yourself the wonderful truth that somewhere deep inside of you is a person designed by God. There can be no path more fulfilling than the one that uses your unique gifts as God intended.

Prayer

Lord, I may be confused about choices I face. I may have given up on who I am, but I want to open my heart to understanding my LifeKeys. *Show me how discovering the ways in which You created me can guide me to a more fulfilling life. Protect me from being side-tracked by my doubts or past failures. Instead, let me grasp how I have been fearfully and wonderfully made by You. Amen.*

---

[4]Keith Miller and Bruce Larson, *The Passionate People* (Waco, Tex.: Word Books, 1979), p. 14.

LifeKey 2

Doing what comes naturally is part of God's plan.

CHAPTER 2

LIFE GIFTS—DOING WHAT COMES NATURALLY

. . . God has already revealed His will to us concerning our vocation and Mission, by causing it to be "written in our members." We are to begin deciphering our unique Mission by studying our talents and skills, and more particularly which ones (or one) we most rejoice to use.[1]

—Richard N. Bolles

Can You Really Be Anything?

"You can be anything you want to be when you grow up if you just work hard at it." Have you heard that line? In many ways it may be true, but there are some limitations. Could you, for example, tour as a concert pianist? Not if your hands aren't big enough to stretch for the chords that are required in some of the great concertos. Could you play trumpet with a famous jazz trio? Not unless your embouchure (mouth position) is correct, no matter how much you practice. Obviously, only a few of us could ever perform with the Metropolitan Opera—or even sing the National Anthem before a televised ball game. There are some things we cannot do, no matter how hard we work at them.

There are other things that simply do not capture our interests, whether we could learn to do them well or not. For example, Jane will never become a tree surgeon—too many tools and too few

---

[1]Bolles, *What Color Is Your Parachute?*, p. 458. Copyright © 1996 by Richard N. Bolles. Used with permission.

people. Sandra has no plans to go into tax accounting—too much detail and not enough variety. David probably would resist being an air traffic controller—too much focused attention!

But the things we are interested in and do well—what a different story! Each of us has found a *LifeKey* to the way God has gifted us.

- Jane can look back to childhood and see overstuffed bookshelves. She often asked her teachers to let her write stories to show what she had learned. Later she chose to major in English in college—so it is no surprise that she is a writer.
- Sandra began teaching Sunday school when she was only a bit older than the children she taught. She gave speeches to raise money to travel as a YMCA youth delegate to Europe—so it is no surprise that her consulting business focuses on training, teaching, and helping others to understand themselves.
- David was president of every school he attended, and even managed to get his fraternity row to organize a Christmas pageant for a local children's home—so it is no surprise that he turned his leadership skills toward helping others through ministry.

We can see how our talents, when combined with our interests—and given certain conditions (family, academic, financial, etc.) in our past—molded each of us into what we do occupationally today. Yet many people assume that they simply "fell into" their life's work. To test this, think of things you could *never* "fall into." Jane couldn't fall into computer programming; Sandra will never operate heavy machinery; and David hasn't the slightest desire to be a dentist. Your natural bents are something you *can* find. If you discover these inclinations, what we will call your *life gifts*, then you can find the things that you enjoy and will most likely do well. Sounds easy, doesn't it?

Are Life Gifts Obvious?

Unfortunately, the way our society views the concept of giftedness puts roadblocks in our path to discovering our life gifts:

- *Certain gifts get all the glory.* We tend to think of only people with athletic ability, artistic talents, and mathematical gifts, for example, as being naturally gifted. Life gifts, however, cover a much broader range than this. Because of our cultural biases, if you happen to be gifted in listening to others or in observing details, you could go through life without ever thinking of yourself as being "gifted."

- *We tend to recognize gifts in others more readily than we see them in ourselves.* To add to this, we often downplay our life gifts because they come so easily to us. We assume everyone can do certain things with the same ease that we can when we are using our life gifts. Therefore we fail to recognize our own special talents and interests as being *special.* For example, Jane's mother never thought much of her wonderful ability to proof-read—until she saw how her daughter, the writer, was incapable of spotting the same errors! Sandra thought everyone could give an impromptu presentation because that was her favorite way to present—until she taught a course in presentations and saw how others struggled.

Does God Really Give Life Gifts?

Each of us has life gifts, chosen by God to fit perfectly with an overall design He has for us. Proverbs 22:6 points out our design:

> Train children in the right way, and when old, they will not stray. (NRSV)

In the past you may have heard this verse as a guarantee: teach your children the truths of Christianity and even if they rebel for a while, eventually they will come back to the fold. But there is another, perhaps more *accurate* meaning. There is a *right* way we *should* go, and it is different for each of us. The Amplified Bible translates the same verse as:

> Train up a child in the way he should go [and in keeping with his individual gift or bent], and when he is old he will not depart from it.

According to Webster's, a bent is "1. a strong inclination or interest. 2. a special inclination or capacity: talent."[2] We are de-

---

[2] *Webster's New Collegiate Dictionary* (Springfield, Mass.: G. & C. Merriam Company, 1977), p. 103.

scribing that *bent* as your *life gift*.

God intended for us to have different life gifts for many different purposes. The building of the first tabernacle is a good example. As the Israelites began their forty-year wandering in the wilderness after being led out of Egypt, God commanded that they make a sanctuary for Him so that He could dwell among them. This sanctuary, or tabernacle, was to be a mobile yet beautifully symbolic structure. God not only gave exacting instructions about the building design, but also revealed the specific people who had the life gifts to do various parts of the work. (The Bible here is using the word "skill" in the manner in which we have defined life gifts—God-given inclinations or bent.)

> Then Moses said to the Israelites: See, the LORD has called by name Bezalel son of Uri son of Hur, of the tribe of Judah; he has filled him with divine spirit, with skill, intelligence, and knowledge in every kind of craft, to devise artistic designs, to work in gold, silver, and bronze, in cutting stones for setting, and in carving wood, in every kind of craft. And he has inspired him to teach, both him and Oholiab son of Ahisamach, of the tribe of Dan. He has filled them with skill to do every kind of work done by an artisan or by a designer or by an embroiderer in blue, purple and crimson yarns, and in fine linen, or by a weaver—by any sort of artisan or skilled designer.
>
> Bezalel and Oholiab and every skillful one to whom the LORD has given skill and understanding to know how to do any work in the construction of the sanctuary shall work in accordance with all that the LORD has commanded. (Exodus 35:30—36:1, NRSV)

Clearly here the life gifts came from God, for His purposes. These workers also used their life gifts in other arenas, even for their livelihood, but God knew that He had provided some of His people with the skills needed just for this moment. The rest of the story relates that the tabernacle was so beautiful and intricate that the Israelites were inspired to give abundantly to the project. Moses finally had to ask them to stop giving because the project was overfunded! The life gifts of the artisans provided blessings to the entire nation.

Why Determine Your Life Gifts?

Knowing your life gifts, whether they show themselves in forms of communication, problem solving, time management, etc., can help you focus your energy on the areas God intended for you. This is knowledge that can keep you from a lot of frustration! Much of our life satisfaction will come from doing what comes naturally—using our unique blend of life gifts. None of us wants to train in vain to be a concert pianist if God designed us to build cathedrals.

Life gifts are not just proficiencies gathered along the way. They are interests God designed specifically for you. For example, are you a problem solver? All of us at one time had to learn basic algebra, but only some of us have a life gift for problem solving that allows us to apply those algebraic principles years later. Or are you able to create things? While in school, most of us were required to make things like a wooden spoon rack in shop or a simple dress in home economics. However, today only a few of us are interested in building furniture or designing and sewing our own clothing.

Many of us are in careers or situations that utilize our life gifts well. If that describes you, then use this chapter for personal confirmation. But because our culture tells us that anyone can succeed at anything if they try hard enough, some of us have pushed ourselves into positions that fit our life gifts no better than a drum can play the melody of a song. Success is far easier when your efforts are in harmony with the life gifts God chose especially for you. God *intended* each of us to have different talents and abilities. He may ask each of us to use these interests at different times of our lives for His purposes.

Are Life Gifts Easy to Identify?

Some people identify their life gifts easily. One geologist could trace her career interests back to the rock collection she started as a preschooler. A top sales representative always outsold his friends in the annual "candy for campers" sales. The task of finding one's life gifts, however, is for some much more difficult.

For example, *the influence of our families may have kept us from exploring the unique gifts God chose for us.* Understandably, we often absorb our parents' interests, values, and sometimes passions.

Separating parental interests from our own interests can be difficult. When we don't do this, we are often propelled into jobs, volunteer organizations, or other situations that may or may not be a good fit for our unique pattern of life gifts.

Some families ignore the "way he should go" part of Proverbs 22:6 and impose their own choice on their child. Perhaps you heard messages, spoken and unspoken, such as, "No child of mine is going to be an artist," or "Since I could never afford the education to become a teacher, you're going to be a teacher because I'll provide the education for you." Others inherit the family business or grow into responsibility on the family farm or simply accept the mantle of their parents' reputation, all without having an opportunity to discover whether that role fits their own life gifts. As adults, we may need to reevaluate the messages our parents transmitted to us about the way we should go.

Others downplay or even bury their life gifts from a fear of appearing proud. They often discount their contributions. They remark, "I made so many mistakes!" when they have just completed a dynamic and nearly perfect marketing presentation. People who bury their life gifts say these things sincerely, not to beg for compliments. They may say, "Oh, it was just luck, I guess" when their life gifts have allowed them to land a big business deal. Perhaps a clue to your life gifts is to consider what you are doing when you feel most lucky! God did not create us only to take the limelight, but think of how our Creator must feel if we never use the tools, the interests, the life gifts that were chosen *just* for us.

Some of us select occupations or tasks based on a distorted self-concept. This misperception of who we are often leads to inappropriate choices or unrealistic ambitions. People who pursue the choices that others have made for them and/or without due regard to their God-given life gifts often experience fatigue or feelings of inadequacy. It takes more energy to do what *doesn't* come naturally. Further, it is much easier to become discouraged because no matter how hard you try, you still may not produce to the level you think you should when you compare yourself to someone who is doing what *does* come naturally. When the proper life gift is absent from the task or situation, you may feel as if it's a drudgery.

What If I'm Good at Something but Don't Really Enjoy It?

Feeling discouraged frequently happens when we mistakenly identify and confuse a skill or competency (learned through experience, training, or education) with a life gift. A good way to think of this is to consider what fruits are yielded through piano lessons. Think of all the children who progress to the easier sonatas and even master a favorite jazz rag or other flashy piece. Multitudes of them still find practicing an effort-filled chore! Compare that to a Mozart, who was composing while still a preschooler and preferred playing music to playing outside. Surely his life gifts fed into and enhanced any skills he developed!

The difference between skills and life gifts can easily become clouded in career choices. Carla spent her freshman year of college carefully evaluating the job market, finally choosing medical technology because of the growing opportunities and probable job security. A good student, she applied herself diligently to each class and landed a choice position before graduation. It wasn't until her children and husband were competing with the medical lab for a limited resource—her energy!—that she realized how little interest her medical technology work held for her. She didn't seem to have the knack or the enthusiasm that some of her colleagues had for intuitively designing research studies or improving diagnostic methods.

Did Carla change careers? Not right away, because she fell into the common trap of thinking that working harder would make things better. Only after much soul-searching did Carla realize that her early success was tied to all of the administrative tasks assigned to her when she first joined the lab. These went by the wayside, replaced with pure lab work, when she was promoted. This new self-knowledge allowed her to select a second career—in hospital management—that matched her life gifts.

Can you see the pattern?

- Practical considerations led to career choice.
- Diligence led to scholastic and early career success.
- Early success led to enhanced responsibilities.
- Life changes led to less energy and enthusiasm.
- Evaluation of the original choice through the framework of life gifts helped identify the mismatch and possible better choices.

You may know someone or may *be* someone who through a similar fate found yourself in a career or situation where you struggle with the responsibilities assigned to you or with another person's expectations for you. Once, however, you identify your true bent—your life gifts—you may be able to readjust your work environment so that you spend more of your time in ways that use your own life gifts. Possibly, even, you will find you need to change your situation entirely. You can make this drastic step less anxiety-ridden by discovering your unique combination of life gifts and acting on that information.

If These Are My Gifts, What Next?

Carla's discovery that she was operating outside her life gifts came through three factors: the stress of a growing family (for others it could be major changes in health, or aging, or a traumatic event, etc.); a shift in job responsibilities so that she was using her life gifts less and less; and a feeling of burnout. There is a huge difference between consciously putting yourself in a place where you *know* you will struggle to fit in versus anticipating that you will fit in and then not understanding why you feel like a misfit. (It's one thing to struggle at a summer job—like detassling corn or filing papers for weeks on end—that you took for the money and no other reason. It's quite another to train for a career and then not understand why you have become so frustrated.) The more you discover about your life gifts, the more nimble you can become at avoiding those situations.

Once you know your life gifts, you may be able to play to your strengths and thereby reduce or eliminate some sources of stress in your life. In some cases you can delegate to others the things that take extra effort or that hold little interest for you. In other cases you can find ways to develop skills in those areas. Being part of the human race, however, means it doesn't always work to say, "I don't have that gift so I don't have to do that." Lacking a life gift for organization does not give you an excuse to be completely disorganized! Nor can you discharge yourself from managing others if you happen to be a parent—you have to manage your children even if you don't want to be a manager at work.

Frequently, though, understanding your life gifts can help you better position yourself. One man whose work involved facilitating seminars found himself growing more and more frustrated. He felt inadequate teaching large groups since he could not sense whether he was helping each person. He finally realized that he worked best when counseling individuals. Eventually, he changed careers and found fulfillment.

A banker who had always thought she had a good head for figures discovered herself mired in the task of computerizing the bank's yearly budget. She had designed an excellent automated system but lacked a life gift for working with details. When she realized the nature of her struggle, she kept responsibility for design and implementation and turned over the data entry and validation process to an individual who was great at finding needles in haystacks.

Another individual inherited a family business her father had headed. After several years of struggling with sluggish sales, she realized that persuasion was not one of her life gifts. Hiring a sales and marketing manager allowed her to concentrate her efforts on manufacturing, human resources, and strategic planning, areas where her life gifts were utilized.

In each of these cases, the people were able to concentrate their efforts on what they naturally did well, turning over to others the areas where they lacked life gifts. In some cases it may be necessary to find ways to compensate by developing a needed skill.

Does Everyone *Really* Have Life Gifts?

Is it difficult for you to believe that you have *any* life gifts? Perhaps when you were a child, the adults in your life never let you know that you—just as you are—were of value to God, to them, or to anyone else. Or maybe bruises from past failures or the impossible standards others set for you or you set for yourself leave you afraid to try anything new. A lack of self-esteem may mean you struggle to convince yourself that you even have life gifts or that they are worth using. Your gifts are there! We ask that you take your concerns in prayer to the One best able to reassure you, the God who gave you these life gifts.

If these doubts reflect your current inner conflict, you are in good company. The Bible is full of people who didn't understand their life gifts until God in some way gave them new insights. The apostle Peter, busy with his fishing boat, had no idea his speeches could rouse others to action. Mary, the sister of Martha, had no idea that her ability to give all her attention to Jesus' words was something that others struggled to do. Martha had no idea that she was loved whether she labored in the kitchen or not. If you find yourself saying, "But I don't . . ." or "Not me . . ." trust as you explore your interests that perhaps your life's path up to this point has detoured past what comes to you naturally. Keep going—we maintain that there *will* be things that interest you. Those are clues to how God has gifted you, to the way you should go.

A Framework for Finding Your Special Life Gifts

Let's take a fresh look at the things you do that energize you, where your interests lie—that natural bent. For more than seventy years, many people have found answers through theoretical work on career choices, particularly that of John Holland. His theory postulates that the world of work can be broken into six areas of preference—that is, six areas where people tend to cluster as they look for fulfillment through using their life gifts. Holland labeled these areas Realistic [R], Investigative [I], Artistic [A], Social [S], Enterprising [E], and Conventional [C]. People who have similar interests or life gifts tend to enjoy similar work, co-workers, and work environments. Their life gifts often derive from these interests.

Holland pictured the relationship between these areas by diagraming them as a hexagon:

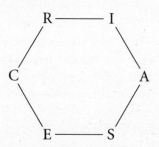

In this hexagon, *R*'s have more in common with *I*'s and *C*'s, which neighbor *R* on the hexagon, than they do with *S*'s, which are farthest away on the hexagon and have the most dissimilar interests. Many people are actually a blend of two and sometimes three of the six areas, adding richness to the workplace.

Typically, people find that their interests, when prioritized, reflect this similarity. One or two of their interest areas generally lie next to each other on the hexagon model. Sometimes, however, an atypical pattern occurs—that is, someone has interests in opposite areas, such as *R* and *S*. While this pattern is normal, it is less common.

What follows is a brief description of each of the six areas, indicating common interests, characteristics, and life gifts of each group. There is a hexagon chart on pages 52–53 for you to keep track of the areas that interest you most. If you want to dig deeper, the *Strong Interest Inventory*™³ is a widely available instrument that can help you identify the areas that fit you best.

Take some time to explore the following descriptions to see which sound like you. As you ponder these and other exercises, don't look for what you *should* be or what you *wish* you were. Look for who you *are*—celebrating what God built into you, discovering the greatest joy of your heart. At the end of the chapter we will look at how you can use this information about your life gifts.

The Realistic Type—"Let's Roll Up Our Sleeves and Get It Done!"

"Outdoorsy," "athletic," "mechanical," "hands-on" are just a few of the words that describe the Realistic type. Few Realistics choose to spend their time at major society events—and they may also resist being behind a desk! Many appear to be "loners," pre-

---

³Published by Consulting Psychologists Press, Palo Alto, CA. If you wish to take the Strong Interest Inventory,™ which matches your interest patterns with those of people in diverse occupations, contact your local community college or the publisher at 800–624–1765.

ferring the company of one or two carefully chosen friends to large-group activities.

Realistic children typically can be found building superhighways in the sandbox, climbing trees, or maybe training a dog or two. One boy was fascinated by anything on wheels from the age of three. His parents let him celebrate one birthday with a visit to a truck dealership. He eventually joined the Army Reserve, where he could drive jeeps and equipment vans every other weekend.

School can be frustrating for Realistics if practical applications of what they are learning aren't clear. They prefer hands-on experiments, concrete problems to solve, and maybe a double dose of physical education or industrial arts. Without these elements, or a teacher who can help them understand future uses of what they are learning, they may long to be elsewhere—especially outside.

These interests lead Realistics to choose careers in agriculture, engineering, construction, for example—careers that let them use their large and fine motor skills to produce tangible results, that allow for pragmatic approaches to problems, and where the work is focused on things rather than on people, ideas, or data. They often seek to provide safety and order, as in military and police work.

In their spare time, Realistics like to enjoy the out-of-doors, even if they spend that time just attending to home maintenance tasks. Many own recreational vehicles, sporting goods, and whatever tools they might need to get a job done.

Typical life gifts include

- mechanical aptitude
- operating heavy equipment, driving, piloting
- manual dexterity
- building mechanical/structural devices
- physical coordination
- organizing supplies or implements
- taking physical risks
- emotional stability, reliability

(If you are a Realistic and doubt that these are life *gifts* that set you apart from others, think of how often you are amazed that others don't *want* to or would actually *pay* someone else to change the oil in their car or strip furniture!)

The Investigative Type—"Let's Figure This Out!"

"Curious," "rational," "intellectual," "introspective," perhaps a "loner"—many people who fit this description have Investigative interests. As the name implies, they want to find out all they can, not settle for simple answers.

Many Investigatives spend their childhood with their nose in a book, in a library, or in the great outdoors where they can observe phenomena for themselves. Most are never satisfied with only *asking* why; they observe, experiment, and analyze until they figure it out. They may be attracted to complicated games such as chess, or to amassing and classifying a collection of fossils or butterflies. One woman spent her adolescence with her eyes on the sky, studying astronomy. She built her own telescope from a kit, spent much of her allowance on books on the subject, and belonged to a stargazing society. To no one's surprise, as an adult she chose a career in scientific research. Investigatives tend to be independent, choosing their own paths. They may seem reserved around others because of their preoccupation with understanding the subjects that interest them.

In school, Investigatives generally have special interests in scientific and mathematical topics and enjoy researching and gathering information. They persevere in solving problems, are adept at collecting and studying data, and prefer to design their own work. Many choose higher education because of a love of knowledge for its own sake. Most Investigatives like working with ideas rather than working with people. This doesn't mean they dislike others, but simply that they would rather discover a cure for cancer than work directly with cancer patients.

41

Investigatives tend to choose careers in the sciences, higher education, or in the more theoretical areas of business such as long-range planning or market research.

Complex activities such as skiing, mountain climbing, spelunking, or sailing, where technology and skill play a major role, are typical hobbies chosen by Investigatives. If they own a computer they know how it works and how to optimize its performance! For Investigatives, work and play are one and the same.

Typical life gifts for Investigative types include

- inventing
- researching
- conceptualizing
- working independently
- solving complex problems
- computer aptitude
- synthesizing information
- theorizing

The Artistic Type—"Let's Create!"

Artistic types look for creative ways of self-expression and are often described as "original," "free-spirited," "creative," and "artistic" or "musical."

Many Artistic children display gifted imaginations (although adults may label this pastime as daydreaming) and create new and novel things, stories, ideas, or ways of being. Depending on their artistic bent, they tend to seek out opportunities to express their gifts at an early age. They may also have a love for visiting art museums or attending musical and theatrical performances. One musician remembers that as a child he grasped any opportunity to perform. He enjoyed being a camp counselor more for the chances to play his guitar than for the work he did with the children.

At school, Artistics do best when allowed to "color outside the lines." They prefer to add their own touch to assignments and feel stifled if required to stick to specifications. Additionally, many Artistics have a natural verbal/linguistic bent that allows them to easily express themselves in writing. When the subject matter or teacher is interesting to them, they tend to do well in school.

For careers, Artistics seek positions that have less structure than most typical businesses. Environments such as law firms, museums, libraries, galleries, interior design consulting, or advertising agencies often allow them to use their life gifts. They may prefer working alone or with one or two others. Those with writing, musical, or artistic life gifts *may* struggle with making a living wage using those talents and therefore *might* choose to use them avocationally.

Leisure pursuits for the Artistic mirror their life gifts. They especially enjoy listening to, seeing, or appreciating their own artistic gifts or those of others.

Typical life gifts for Artistic types include

- acting
- writing, reporting, technical writing
- verbal/linguistics skills
- musical expression
- creative problem solving
- sculpting/photography/graphic arts/painting
- creative design through use of space
- creative expression through color

(Note that Artistic interests go far beyond the sculpting or painting of those we think of as "artists." Reporters, librarians, and others also have the type of creative bent that reflects Artistic interests.)

The Social Type—"Let's Work on This Together!"

Social types can be described as "helpful," "cooperative," "understanding," and "people-oriented." Many would rather work in a group than alone and are interested in the well-being as well as the development of others. (Compare this with our description of Realistics to appreciate the diversity of these natural bents.)

As children, most Social types are well-liked because they tend to be accepting of others and have natural people skills. They often become involved in social concerns at an early age. Sandra remembers trying to garner support at her church to start a shelter for stray animals. Jane spent a summer organizing bake sales and talent shows to raise money for a children's charity foundation. Many Social children become deeply involved in religious organizations, connecting with the people- and service-oriented atmosphere.

Most Socials look forward to school because of the friendships they develop. They learn best in groups where they can work cooperatively and enjoy passing on to others what they have learned. They may prefer the humanities or social sciences to more scientific subjects.

Many Socials choose careers where they can serve others, preferring to work for schools, religious institutions, social services, health organizations, or in parts of business organizations that focus on people, such as customer service. They enjoy environments where problems are resolved through cooperation.

In their spare time, many Socials choose to entertain others or do volunteer work. Because Socials focus so heavily on the needs of people, which can be draining, they may choose Realistic activities for their leisure time to avoid burnout.

Typical life gifts for the Social type include

- teaching
- listening and facilitating
- understanding or counseling others
- conversing/informing
- serving
- evaluating people's character
- showing empathy and tact
- working with others

The Enterprising Type—"Let's Get Going!"

Enterprising types are frequently described as "persuasive," "self-confident," "extroverted," and "risk-takers." They often gravitate toward leadership positions and are perhaps more interested in the power and prestige that goes along with leadership than the other types. They enjoy promoting and selling products and people, themselves included.

Many Enterprising types report childhoods filled with paper routes, student leadership positions, and other hints of industry to come. In college, David convinced his father to let him have the smaller trees from the family tree farm to sell on campus. He and his partners made enough selling dorm-room-sized Christmas trees to treat themselves to a great lobster dinner. Enterprising types want to enjoy the fruits of their labor and may work hard to attain certain possessions that are regarded as status symbols.

In school, Enterprising types may spend a lot of time figuring out how to work around the system. One Enterprising type persuaded his social studies teacher to count his run for class president as his independent project for the term. While they can be excellent students, they tend to dislike long academic pursuits or scientific efforts.

If Enterprisers don't become entrepreneurs, many of them choose careers in sales, elected government positions, brokerage (real estate, travel), or fundraising activities. They like to set monetary or advancement goals for themselves and often enjoy pursuing those goals as much or more than achieving them. They quickly move on to a new set of goals once they have attained their objective.

In their spare time, Enterprising types may pursue political activities or leadership in community organizations. They also enjoy sporting events where they can see and be seen. The participative sports they choose—like tennis or golf—often reflect a desire to belong to prestigious clubs or social organizations.

Typical Enterprising life gifts include

- public speaking
- selling
- persuading
- leadership
- management
- negotiating
- taking action
- adventurousness

The Conventional Type—"Let's Be Dependable!"

"Practical," "methodical," "efficient," and "orderly" are adjectives that commonly describe people with Conventional life gifts. They are the ones who keep life running smoothly for everyone else with their bent for detail and accuracy. They are a blessing for those who can't keep track of their car keys, let alone organize their office.

Many Conventional children enjoy structured activities such as scouting and youth organizations, school or community-sponsored leagues, and games with prescribed rules. They frequently have the cleanest room in the family and take exceptionally good care of their belongings. One woman still has every piece of her *cardboard* Barbie dollhouse and car from 1959, all pieces in mint condition. She played with it constantly but carefully put each piece away in the same manner at the close of each play session. Her meticulous habits help identify her Conventional bent.

School subjects that require mastery of set rules are often favorites for Conventional children. They tend to like arithmetic and spelling, where they can easily chart their progress. They may struggle with school subjects that require heavy use of theory, intuition, or creativity, preferring topics that have concrete answers.

Conventional types often choose accounting, office management, data processing, and other structured fields where careful handling of data and detail is important. They tend to prefer set schedules and routines and may add these qualities to environments where they work.

In their spare time, many Conventionals choose to vacation in familiar places such as a family cabin or seaside resort where they can renew old acquaintances and seek rest in customary surroundings. They may enjoy hobbies such as china collecting or building detailed models such as railroads, dollhouses, or motorized airplanes.

Typical Conventional life gifts include

- organizing
- appraising/evaluating
- attending to detail
- managing time, setting priorities
- calculating and mathematical skills
- systematizing
- persistence
- stewardship

Choose Your Themes; Find Your Life Gifts

Now that you've journeyed through the six areas of interest, identify those (at least one but no more than three) that describe you best, abbreviating them by their first letters. Jane, for example, is an SAI, Sandra an AES, and David an EIS. If you are unsure, many people find it helpful to sort the cartoons above each description into the order of priority for them. Write your own theme code below:

——— ——— ———

These are the "home fields" where you can begin the process of identifying your life gifts. Not everyone has all of the life gifts listed under each area. In addition, someone can have life gifts in areas other than his or her home field. Your interest theme, though, is a great place to start the search for your natural bent.

The next part of this section contains six pages, one for each interest area. *Beginning with the page for the area you chose as your natural bent,* answer the questions for those gifts you believe may be your life gifts. Then continue through the interest areas in their order of priority to you.

You may sum up your life gifts by highlighting them on the hexagon chart on pages 52–53. Also, record them in LifeKeys Notations, page 239, a place where you can summarize your discoveries.

If this process seems too simple, consider the following:

- You may never have really stopped to consider what you do best, other than the obvious.
- You may have so smoothly integrated some of your life gifts into your daily life that you have never recognized their uniqueness.
- You may have life gifts that you never realized others struggle with—you thought everyone could handle those tasks as easily as you do.

These exercises help you organize your thoughts about what to you may be second nature. We have two other suggestions before you begin:

1. Remember to consider the life gifts outside of your theme codes. Jane is SAI but has the Conventional life gift of managing time and priorities. David is EIS but has the Realistic life gift of taking physical risks. Sandra is AES but has the Investigative gift of synthesizing the research of others.

2. There is a difference between being attracted to an area and being truly interested in that area. For example, many children may say they want to play soccer, but few are out every day after school practicing their ball-handling skills. For this identification process to be helpful, try to stick to those interests that motivate you to *action*.

Making Your Life Gifts Your Own

As you work your way through these pages, you might say, "Yes! These are my life gifts. So that's why that project went so well. . . ." Or you might be less sure and will need to process what you have learned. You probably already use some of your talents nearly every day. And there may be other life gifts you have never recognized. You may have been on time in every project you have ever undertaken, for example, and not realized that such organization is a natural bent.

If you are unsure about some of your life gifts, here are some suggestions:

a. Ask friends, co-workers, or others close to you about whether they have seen you operate using the life gifts you identified through the exercises. Encourage them to give you specific examples.

b. Observe others using the life gifts you have identified for yourself. Ask yourself whether what they are doing is something you could do.

c. Volunteer for a task that will allow you to use a possible life gift. If you can, ask someone you trust to give you honest feedback on your performance.

d. Brainstorm on how you might use each life gift, both in your current life and in the future. A retiree might use a life gift for selling to raise funds for a project, recruit volunteers, or gather support for a new program. A student might use a tutoring life gift as a volunteer with children or as an assistant coach. A mother might use a life gift for listening to facilitate family discussions, work out parent-teacher organization issues, or be a part of a church's care-giving ministry. Each life gift can be used in a variety of circumstances.

Working with Your Life Gifts—Forming a Melody

Discovering your life gifts, a part of you since birth, is an exciting process for many people, but some of you may be asking, "Where do I go from here?" Use the following exercise to link your life gifts into a sentence or series of phrases that will help you remember not only what your life gifts are, but how they often work together.

David wrote out his life gift list as follows after working through pages 54–59.

1. Taking risks
2. Researching
3. Synthesizing
4. Acting
5. Listening and facilitating
6. Teaching
7. Public speaking

8. Selling
9. Leadership
10. Being of service

While a list is helpful, linking these life gifts in a sentence helps David's natural bent come alive in a dramatic way. David asked himself the following three questions:

1. Which life gifts are used the most often and are central to who I am? (For David, these were all communication gifts.)
2. Which gifts are normally used first, if applicable, before the other gifts are used?
3. Which gifts are used normally after the others are used?

Through his answers to these questions, David came up with a statement that explains much of his chosen activity:

I list, interview, investigate, and research in order to synthesize and organize information. I then take the information to teach, train, promote, persuade, speak, or act so that I might be of service to people, especially in the areas of interpersonal risk.

Work with your list of life gifts and see if you can construct a similar statement that links them together into a coherent picture. Don't worry about using every gift or about having sentences that link together easily. The point here is to create phrases or sentences that help you understand how your life gifts work together.

Prayer

Dear God,

It is often beyond my understanding that because of Your love for each one of us, You took the effort to gift us individually with our own natural bents—our life gifts, the way we should go.

Help me enjoy the process of finding my life gifts. Guard me from comparing mine to those of others or worrying about which ones I would rather have. Reassure me that You have made me this way for Your purposes. In that confidence I can rejoice. Amen.

HEXAGON OF INTEREST AREAS WITH ASSOCIATED LIFE GIFTS

Realistic

Mechanical aptitude
Operating heavy equipment,
    driving, piloting
Manual dexterity
Building mechanical/structural devices
Physical coordination (athletics, etc.)
Organizing supplies or equipment
Taking risks, especially physical
Emotional stability, reliability

R

Conventional

Organizing records, finances, offices,
    production lines, homes, etc.
Appraising/evaluating
Attending to detail
Managing time, setting priorities
Calculating and mathematical skills
Systematizing and classifying
    information or things for ease of use
Persistence, follow-through and patience
Stewardship with conservative
    handling of data, things and people

C

Enterprising

Public speaking
Selling/purchasing
Persuading/advocating
Leadership
Managing projects to meet goals
Promoting/supplying ambition
    and energy to tasks and people
Being decisive
Adventuresome: taking financial
    and interpersonal risks

E

Investigative

Inventing, especially in technical, scientific
or theoretical realms
Researching, investigating
Conceptualizing
Working independently
Solving complex problems
Computer aptitude, especially software
design and development
Synthesizing information, organizing
research so others can understand it
Theorizing, finding connections or
projecting the future

I

Artistic

Acting
Writing, reporting,
technical writing
Verbal/linguistics skills
Musical
Creative problem solving
Sculpting/photography/graphic
arts/painting
Designing/composing
Creative expression through
color or design

A

S

Social

Teaching, demonstrating, training others
Listening and facilitating
Understanding or counseling others
Conversing/informing
Being of service: considering the welfare of others
Evaluating people's character
Being empathetic and tactful
Organizing social gatherings

Realistic Life Gifts

Life Gifts	When have I used this? Or have I dreamed about using this?	How enjoyable were these experiences (1=terrible, 10=great)	How easy or difficult is it for me to use?	Could this be a life gift?
Mechanical aptitude—able to understand and apply the principles of mechanics and physics				
Operating heavy equipment, driving, piloting—construction equipment as well as transportation vehicles				
Manual dexterity—skill and ease at using one's hands or fine tools				
Building mechanical/ structural devices—able to design and/or assemble materials as well as execute repairs				
Physical coordination—using multiple muscle movements to a single end, such as needed in athletics, skilled trades, etc.				
Organizing supplies or implements—able to identify methods that lead to ease of retrieval and maintenance				
Taking physical risks—attracted to activities or occupations with elements of physical danger				
Emotional stability, reliability—able to react impersonally to situations and thereby stay on course				

Investigative Life Gifts

Life Gifts	When have I used this? Or have I dreamed about using this?	How enjoyable were these experiences (1=terrible, 10=great)	How easy or difficult is it for me to use?	Could this be a life gift?
Inventing—to imagine or produce something useful, especially in technical, scientific, or theoretical realms				
Researching—investigating or experimenting to get information, examine theories, or find new applications of current knowledge				
Conceptualizing—originating and developing abstract ideas or theories				
Working independently—able to work well without guidance or input from others				
Solving complex problems—able to find solutions to difficult situations or unique issues, usually through logic or knowledge base				
Computer aptitude—adept at systems and software design and development				
Synthesizing information—organizing or combining information from different sources so that it is easily understood				
Theorizing—articulating explanations, finding connections, or projecting future trends				

Artistic Life Gifts

Life Gifts	When have I used this? Or have I dreamed about using this?	How enjoyable were these experiences (1=terrible, 10=great)	How easy or difficult is it for me to use?	Could this be a life gift?
Acting—projecting emotions or character by performing roles, either formally in theater settings or informally				
Writing, reporting, technical writing—able to communicate clearly through written words, including reports, letters, and publications				
Verbal/linguistics skills—adept at studying or learning languages, using and comprehending spoken words				
Musical expression—able to compose music or perform musically, either with voice, body, or instruments				
Creative problem solving—able to find unusual solutions to issues, especially in artistic or interpersonal areas				
Sculpting/photography/graphic arts/painting—creative expression through artistic mediums				
Creative design through use of space—able to work with spatial concepts, as in interior design or architecture				
Creative expression through color—able to coordinate colors and patterns, as in clothing design, decorating, etc.				

Social Life Gifts

Life Gifts	When have I used this? Or have I dreamed about using this?	How enjoyable were these experiences (1=terrible, 10=great)	How easy or difficult is it for me to use?	Could this be a life gift?
Teaching—instructing, demonstrating, training, or guiding the study of others so that they can learn facts or concepts				
Listening and facilitating—able to encourage others to volunteer information and discuss issues or topics, either one-on-one or in groups				
Understanding or counseling others—able to give appropriate advice and guidance tailored to the needs of others				
Conversing/informing—offering hospitality, talking and listening informally with one or a few others about daily events, issues, or personal concerns				
Serving—considering and acting to aid the welfare of others				
Evaluating people's character—able to discern the motives and values of other people				
Showing empathy and tact—aware of the feelings of others, able to adjust one's own behavior and respond accordingly				
Working with others—able to establish harmonious working relationships based on trust and synergy				

Enterprising Life Gifts

Life Gifts	When have I used this? Or have I dreamed about using this?	How enjoyable were these experiences (1=terrible, 10=great)	How easy or difficult is it for me to use?	Could this be a life gift?
Public speaking—able to communicate clearly in front of a live audience				
Selling—able to convince others to purchase products or services				
Persuading—advocating the acceptance by others of ideas, values, or points of view				
Leadership—able to influence others to work together and direct people's efforts toward common missions or goals				
Management—planning, organizing, and directing projects and resources to attain goals				
Negotiating—able to aid others in listening to diverse opinions or demands so as to reach agreement or compromise				
Taking action—responding decisively in emergency or stressful situations				
Adventurousness—able to take above-average financial and interpersonal risks				

Conventional Life Gifts

Life Gifts	When have I used this? Or have I dreamed about using this?	How enjoyable were these experiences (1=terrible, 10=great)	How easy or difficult is it for me to use?	Could this be a life gift?
Organizing—able to arrange records, finances, offices, production lines, homes, etc., in a structured manner				
Appraising/evaluating—able to accurately estimate the value or significance of investments, antiques, real estate, business opportunities, etc.				
Attending to detail—aware of the small elements that make up the whole, as in printed words, administrative tasks, or the environment				
Managing time, setting priorities—arranging activities and schedules so that deadlines, appointments, and goals are consistently met				
Calculating and mathematical skills—adept at working with numbers and figures; adding, subtracting, multiplying, dividing				
Systematizing—classifying information or things for ease of use				
Persistence—exhibiting follow-through and patience when handling responsibilities				
Conserving—careful handling of money, data, things, and people				

LifeKey 3

There are no second fiddles in God's orchestra.

CHAPTER 3

SPIRITUAL GIFTS—GOD'S SPECIAL INSTRUMENTS

Each one should use whatever gift he has received to serve others, faithfully administering God's grace in its various forms.

—1 Peter 4:10

If the theme song from *The Twilight Zone* comes to mind at the mention of spiritual gifts, please stay tuned! Spiritual gifts are simply another *LifeKey*, the special instruments God gives for the unique tasks of the Church. Life gifts meet needs in all arenas of life, but spiritual gifts help us carry out a special task: bringing people to God. Given human nature, this is not a simple job; it is a job that cannot be completed without supernatural help.

Many of the instruments God uses are quite ordinary in appearance. For example, teaching is a life gift *and* a spiritual gift. But as a spiritual gift, God tunes *teaching* to a different pitch; conveying spiritual truth as opposed to conveying other truths such as mathematical theories. Many of the instruments God calls spiritual gifts are quiet and unassuming. For instance, those with the gift of *helps* may be playing the background music so harmoniously that they are hardly noticed.

There are, however, a few instruments that cause some controversy—the spiritual gifts that are misunderstood in this day and age or are so rare that few of us are familiar with their sound or purpose. Think of God for a moment as an orchestra conductor standing before a new audience in a strange hall. God wants to get that audience's attention in order to communicate the love He has for them, so this time the orchestra includes a synthesizer, or electric guitars, or unfamiliar oriental instruments, or bagpipes. These aren't used often in the orchestra (can you imagine a bagpipe droning Beethoven's Fifth Symphony?) but when God asks them to play a part, these special instruments—the spiritual gifts—can have an effect that is beautiful, stunning, eye-opening, even staggering to those who hear or experience them.

Some of the spiritual gifts, like some of these more unusual instruments, take some getting used to. Others are so powerful that they must be used sparingly. We need to understand these instruments, the spiritual gifts, to appreciate where and why God calls us to use them.

What Is a Spiritual Gift?

Let's leave that unusual orchestra behind for a moment and come back to it after we understand the more conventional instruments used in God's Church.

> Now to each one the manifestation [revelation, unveiling, evidence, demonstration] of the Spirit is given for the common good. (1 Corinthians 12:7, *our amplification*)

Spiritual gifts, then, are *evidence* or a *demonstration* that God's Holy Spirit is working in us, enabling us to do things we could not otherwise do.

Knowing what our spiritual gifts are can help steer us to the right places to give and to serve. Did you ever volunteer for a task or a ministry only to find that your willingness was a major mistake? That happened to Jane and her husband, Brian. Having worked with teens in the past, they agreed to chaperone a Christian rock concert. Four hours later they found themselves with severe headaches and a nagging feeling that they had aged way beyond their years. They had little energy left for leading the encounter groups for teens who chose to stay after the music ended. Afterward, Jane and Brian agreed that they lacked the gifts of *encouragement* and *evangelism* to work with youth in this way! After this experience they stuck to *teaching*.

One young mother willingly assumed the missions coordinator post that her friend had previously held. Not only did this mother feel overwhelmed once she saw how well organized her friend had been, but the job's tasks were not fulfilling to her—they called for gifts of *administration* rather than the tangible acts of *mercy* that she did so well.

What conductor would lead an orchestra the way we approach too many recruitment efforts or the way we choose our own places to serve? *Hmmm*, the drums did such a great job keeping the beat last week—let's give them the melody for "The Blue Danube." And the strings? Well, the bows would make great drumsticks. The cellos can be the timpani and the . . .

None of us would lead an orchestra that way, yet too often that is how we act at church—we ask people to serve, or we volunteer ourselves without finding out what each of us does best. God has a better plan. God is a giver of gifts to build us up for ministry to the world.

The early Church continually saw spiritual gifts in action, but they were confused about how they should use the gifts. In a letter to the church at Corinth, where the gifts were causing harsh disagreements, Paul tried to explain:

> There are different kinds of gifts, but the same Spirit. There are different kinds of service, but the same Lord. There are different kinds of working, but the same God works all of them in all [people].
>
> Now to each one the manifestation of the Spirit is given for the common good. To one there is given through the Spirit the message of *wisdom*, to another the message of *knowledge* by means of the same Spirit, to another *faith* by the same Spirit, to another gifts of *healing* by that one Spirit, to another *miraculous powers*, to another *prophecy*, to another the ability to *distinguish between spirits*, to another the ability to speak in different kinds of *tongues*, and to still another the *interpretation of tongues*. All these are the work of one and the same Spirit, and he gives them to each [one], just as he determines. (1 Corinthians 12:4–11, *emphasis ours*)

Paul makes three crucial points:

1. All believers have been given spiritual gifts by the Holy Spirit. These gifts are offered so that the Body of Christ has what it needs to spread God's message of love. They are not given for the benefit of the individual who receives them; we are simply stewards of the gifts we are given. Whatever gifts we have are for the common good, not for our own glorification.

2. God distributes the gifts among believers according to His will, not because of some effort on our part. For example, in the early Church, God saw a great way to spread the gospel to the Gentiles: by gifting Paul, to the amazement of many whom Paul had persecuted. Paul was one of the greatest evangelists and teachers in the history of the Church, yet in human eyes he probably deserved *no* gifts, given his early violence toward Christians.

Christian maturity is shown not by spiritual gifts but by the fruit of the Spirit such as love, peace, and patience. The familiar start to 1 Corinthians 13, "If I speak in the tongues of men and of angels, but have not love, I am only a resounding gong or a clanging cymbal," (v. 1) points out the dissonance that can result from using spiritual gifts unaccompanied by the love and joy that are gained through Christian maturity.

3. In the Body of Christ, each of us has something to contribute. If for some reason we choose not to use the gifts God gave us, the Church will be less than it could have been. Therefore, each individual and his or her unique contribution counts.

Spiritual gifts, understood within the context of these principles, can allow the Church to achieve its highest goals.

Me?? Gifts??

Many Christians are either unaware of their spiritual gifts, have left them dormant for a long time, or doubt if they really exist. As they think about spiritual gifts they may conclude either that they have none or that their gifts are less worthy than the gifts God has given others. Paul strongly refutes this:

> The eye cannot say to the hand, "I don't need you!" And the head cannot say to the feet, "I don't need you!" On the contrary, those parts of the body that seem to be weaker are indispensable, and the parts that we think are less honorable we treat with special honor. And the parts that are unpresentable are treated with special modesty, while our presentable parts need no special treatment. But God has combined the members of the body and has given greater honor to the parts that lacked it, so that there should be no division in the

body, but that its parts should have equal concern for each other. If one part suffers, every part suffers with it; if one part is honored, every part rejoices with it. (1 Corinthians 12:21–26)

Biblically, Paul leaves no doubt that we all have spiritual gifts and that each person and each gift is important. God has given you a specific gift or gifts so that the Church may be complete. Picture yourself as a vital element in God's plan for the Church, because that is what you are. You are a special mix of spiritual gifts and life gifts that God has chosen uniquely for you:

Now here is what I am trying to say: All of you together are the one body of Christ and each one of you is a separate and necessary part of it. (1 Corinthians 12:27, TLB)

Aren't the Gifts Just for Leaders?

Another common reaction of believers is to assume that a person with several of the more public spiritual gifts, such as *leadership* and *teaching*, can manage things just fine alone. Frequently these gifts are viewed as more important because they are so visible:

Suppose the whole body were an eye—then how would you hear? Or if your whole body were just one big ear, how could you smell anything?

But that isn't the way God has made us. He has made many parts for our bodies and has put each part just where he wants it. What a strange thing a body would be if it had only one part! So he has made many parts, but still there is only one body. (1 Corinthians 12: 17–20, TLB)

If you have ever worked with a Christian who tried to lead alone, you may have witnessed less than wonderful results. Perhaps a visionary ministry led by someone with the gift of *apostleship* falters because of inherent disorganization; someone with the gift of *administration* may have helped bring order to the chaos. Maybe an *evangelism* outreach fails because people don't connect with others who could help them grow in faith; someone with the gift of *shepherding* might have found places for them to connect. Maybe an education class falls short of its goal because the materials weren't ready, upsetting the *teacher;* someone with the gift of *helps* could have solved the problem. God makes it clear every day how much we need each other.

A worse situation can arise when a congregation sits back because of an unexamined belief that their pastor can do everything. That pastor may eventually become exhausted and feel defeated by the congregation's endless needs.

A church that understands the spiritual gifts of its people can move forward as a group of mutually *interdependent*, mutually *accepting*, mutually *supportive*, and mutually *synergistic* people serving together under the lordship of Christ. For this to happen, individuals need to bring the variety of their spiritual gifts to the work of the Church. This is a part of God's plan for building His kingdom on earth.

Supernatural or Sensational—What's the Difference?

You may not have realized that you are already using spiritual gifts. While all of the gifts are *supernatural*, coming through the Holy Spirit and enabling us to do more than we could do on our own, not all of them are *sensational*, that is, enough out of the ordinary that they astound us when we see them in operation. For example, two retirees saw nothing unusual about the way they had surveyed the trade skills of senior citizens in their congregation and organized a system so that plumbers, painters, electricians, and others could be called on for maintenance projects at church and the ministries they supported. They didn't connect their efforts with their gifts of *leadership* and *administration* until others pointed out that no one else had known how to make this system happen!

Would you place their abilities in the same category as those of a man or woman able to command a wheelchair-bound person to rise and walk—enabling visible *healing* to take place? The latter is more *sensational*, but both a gift to heal and the quieter abilities of the repair crew organizers are *supernaturally* given by God so the work of the Church can go on.

If you want to be a part of God's plan and feel the specialness that is yours alone, believe that you have been given gifts, find out what they are, develop them as best you can, and put them to use!

What Is the Difference Between Life Gifts and Spiritual Gifts?

There is definite overlap in effect between life gifts and spiritual gifts, but life gifts have many applications, while spiritual gifts are given to carry out God's purposes. "It was he who gave some to be *apostles*, some to be *prophets*, some to be *evangelists*, and some to be *pastors* and *teachers, to prepare God's people for works of service*, so that the body of Christ may be built up until we all reach unity in the faith and in the knowledge of the Son of God and become mature, attaining to the whole measure of the fullness of Christ" (Ephesians 4:11–13, *emphasis ours*).

Frequently, but not always, life gifts and spiritual gifts are related. Some but not all Christians with a life gift for public speaking may use that life gift through the spiritual gift of *evangelism*. The same is true with the spiritual gift of *teaching*. Some but not all people with a life gift for teaching will find that they have a spiritual gift for *teaching* that allows them to relay biblical truths to others.

This principle holds true in reverse as well. A spiritual gift may or may not be active as a life gift. Think of pastors with the spiritual gift of *leadership*. How many of them would enjoy a role in business or government? Some, but certainly not all. *Evangelists* may be gifted in persuading others to accept Christianity but may not be gifted in selling anything else.

Even so, a good way to start to discern your spiritual gifts is to look at your life gifts. If you previously listed teaching or persuading or organizing as life gifts, look first at the spiritual gifts of *teaching* or *evangelism* or *administration*. If you aren't sure, there is a great way to find out—volunteer for several tasks. Which ones come easiest to you? Which give you and those you serve the most satisfaction? Remember, the volunteer organizations generally have easy requirements for previous experience!

Are Our Spiritual Gifts Fully Developed When We Receive Them?

Some people think they lack a specific spiritual gift if they cannot practice that gift immediately. However, if asked, many Christians with the spiritual gift of *teaching* will describe how over time they have become more aware of the Holy Spirit's power and depend on it more and more for what they will say. Most of those with the spiritual gift of *leadership* will point to improvements in their communication skills, better planning processes, or other acquired management skills. Those with the gift of *mercy* may relate how special training in counseling or grief support has enabled them to expand their ministry use of this spiritual gift.

Additionally, some are given a fuller measure of a gift than others. Only a few Billy Grahams are necessary, but God needs an infinite number of *evangelists* to share the gospel with others one at a time.

If you are serious about discovering your gifts—especially if the idea of spiritual gifts is new to you or you have limited experience serving within the Church—try to picture yourself using each gift as we describe them. Try to ignore any ideas about which ones are "best" for you or "better" to have and concentrate on those that God has in mind for you.

Do All Spiritual Gifts Operate in the Church Today?

Many Christians are so opposed to the gifts of *healing, miracles,* and *speaking in tongues* that they tend to ignore all spiritual gifts. Yet denying the existence of these particular spiritual gifts leaves us without explanations of many documented events involving *healing, miracles,* and *speaking in tongues* that exist today.

The Spiritual Gift Descriptions included in this chapter give more details about each of the gifts, but the personal experience of one Christian may lend perspective. In the early 1960s, John Sherrill, longtime editor of *Guideposts* magazine, set out to do an objective story on the modern-day use of the gift of tongues. The more he heard, the deeper his confusion. A friend finally pointed out how he was concentrating on the wrong thing. Tongues were an obstacle to Sherrill, blocking him from seeing the workings of the Holy Spirit. His friend likened it to the way a garish red entrance door could detract from the beauty of a Gothic cathedral:

> Tongues, John, are like that door. As long as you stand outside, your attention is going to be riveted there and you're not going to be able to see anything else. Once you go through, however, you are surrounded by the thousand won-

ders of light and sound and form that the architect intended. You look around and that door isn't even red on the inside. It's there. It's to be used. But it has taken its proper place in the design of the whole Church.

That's what I'd hope for you, John. I think it's time for you to walk through that door. If you really want to discover what the Pentecostal experience[1] is all about, don't concentrate on tongues, but step through the door and meet the Holy Spirit.[2]

Don't let yourself be distracted from the true nature of spiritual gifts. Don't worry that God might lead you into an experience you are not ready to handle. While God often challenges our understanding, He gently leads those who are open to His working. In discovering your gifts and finding ways to use them to do God's work, let the same Holy Spirit who has led countless others also be your guide.

Prayer

Dear God,

I believe that You have given spiritual gifts to those of us who seek to carry out Your purposes. Now walk with me as I learn more about each of these gifts and seek to discover which gifts You have given me. Don't let anything distract me, but allow me to "step through the door" and see how I can use them for Your glory. Amen.

Using the Spiritual Gift Descriptions

Each spiritual gift is described below with a teaching or true story of one of our friends or someone from our congregation who uses that gift. The three of us have seen each of these spiritual gifts at work within our congregation, and most likely you will see them within your community of faith as well. As you go through the descriptions, we offer the following hints:

- For many people, their spiritual gifts are already present but they have not yet "unwrapped" them. For this reason, our sto-

---

[1]Meaning, experiencing the Holy Spirit personally.
[2]John Sherrill, *They Speak With Other Tongues* (New York: McGraw Hill, 1964), p. 114.

ries illustrate spiritual gifts at work in the lives of people who have just discovered them, rather than how they might be used by someone who has been using that spiritual gift for years.

- Look at the list of spiritual gifts below. Start by reading the ones that sound most appealing to you or are the most like the life gifts you identified for yourself. *Then read through the rest of the stories.* As you read each story, consider these questions: Do you see yourself in it? Does it remind you of someone you know? If so, jot these things down.

- Read through the common characteristics of a person with that gift and mark the ones you might share. If this subject or service in the Church is new to you, please be kind to yourself! Even if some of the descriptions name things you have never done, please think about them. Do they sound interesting to you? Would you consider trying some of the things mentioned? Can you picture yourself using a particular spiritual gift because it is similar to one of your life gifts? And remember, while the spiritual gifts identified in this manner may not be your actual ones, it does give you a way to start. It suggests places to experiment in volunteer service.

- If you are undecided about a gift, look up the biblical references. Record any new insights you find in these sources.

- Look through the suggestions for developing a spiritual gift. Do any of these sound like a match for you? If so, you might wish to visit with someone in formal or informal leadership at your church about the places available to use each gift—and to ask whether they see this gift operating within you. In what place or volunteer role would you be most comfortable?

After reviewing a spiritual gift, turn to pages 121–122 and record your findings for that gift according to the instructions.

And remember, remain open to the possibility that each spiritual gift may be one that God has given to you to help you find the unique place that God designed you for—your place in His orchestra.

The spiritual gifts we will look at include:

Administration • Apostleship • Discernment
Encouragement/Counseling • Evangelism • Faith • Giving
Healing • Helps • Hospitality • Knowledge • Leadership

Mercy • Miracles • Pastoring/Shepherding • Prophecy
Teaching • Tongues • Interpretation of Tongues • Wisdom

ADMINISTRATION

A person with the gift of administration has the ability to organize information, events, or material to work efficiently for the Body of Christ.

Biblical Reference: "And in the church God has appointed ... those with gifts of administration ...." (1 Corinthians 12:28).

"That sounds like a great project, but there just aren't enough staff resources to cover it right now" was the message that came back to Jeff from the church. Jeff wanted his congregation to sponsor the rebuilding of the playground across the street from their inner-city sister church—and he wanted to see it done before school resumed in just five weeks. While the playground had long needed repairs, six days before, vandals had destroyed most of the useable equipment. The insurance settlement would cover only the cost of materials, not the cleanup and labor needed to make the kind of playground the kids deserved.

As Jeff considered the church staff's reluctance, he thought, "Why should the staff take time away from their other responsibilities? I think I can organize this myself."

His pastor agreed that Jeff could publicize the playground rebuilding needs in the church newsletter and recruit members through the church's usual methods. Jeff methodically listed his needs:

- A plan for the playground
- Coordination of the purchase of all materials, both for equipment and landscaping
- A counterpart to himself at their sister church so that they could provide volunteers as well
- A liaison to ensure that all safety and equal access standards were met

- Volunteers to act as supervisors for the job, preferably two or three so that one could always be present during construction
- Volunteer workers
- Someone to schedule volunteers
- Someone to coordinate delivery of refreshments for workers

Jeff was not a contractor but had been involved with constructing the playground at his own children's school. He quickly contacted the leaders of that job to get the names and numbers of people who could make this project happen in the short time they had. He got a friend to photograph the ruined playground; he then displayed the photos on church bulletin boards to build support for the project. He found a supplier to help them design the playground using only materials that were on hand so that construction would not be delayed by special orders. Jeff contacted the head of the teachers' association at the school, and she in turn organized many of the teachers to volunteer on one of their workshop days.

Jeff never pounded a nail or lifted a board on the playground project—not because he wanted to keep his hands clean, but because the administrative details kept his hands full. He sent out reminder notices, contacted equipment renters, delivered food, and dropped off volunteers. He focused the spotlight on the volunteers, emphasizing what people can do when they mobilize for a task that is bigger than anyone could do alone. He saw himself as an administrator, not a leader. "The project led itself once people recognized the need. I didn't inspire or motivate, I just kept the machinery well oiled," he said when a friend tried to praise his leadership skills.

The spiritual gift of *administration* often acts this way. A person with a life gift for managing time and priorities, finances, or organization simply comes alongside an effort and adds the ingredients needed for God to accomplish His purposes.

Do you have the spiritual gift of administration?

☐ I like to organize facts, people, or events.
☐ When I am working on a project or event, it is easy for me to see the necessary steps in the process to solve potential problems.
☐ I tend to be frustrated when I see disorganization.

☐ I enjoy learning about management issues and how organizations function effectively.

☐ I enjoy using my life gifts of managing time and priorities and/or organization and/or financial management.

☐ I am generally careful and thorough in handling details.

Suggestions for developing your spiritual gift of administration:

1. Observe how others with this gift organize events, outreaches, offices, or other tasks in which you have an interest. Consider where you would be most comfortable helping with a similar event.
2. Develop skills that can improve your efficiency, such as computer expertise, accounting, strategic planning, or proficiency in oral or written communication.
3. If you are unsure whether this is one of your gifts, start by taking administrative responsibility for a small project.

Biblical Example

Joseph (Genesis 41: 33–57)

APOSTLESHIP

A person with the gift of apostleship has the ability to minister transculturally, starting new churches or ministries that impact multiple churches.

Biblical Reference: "But to each one of us grace has been given as Christ apportioned it. . . . It was he who gave some to be apostles . . ." (Ephesians 4:7, 11).

Ed and Linda Garrick started looking for short-term mission opportunities after hearing how much their children had gained from church youth group service trips. As Ed put it, "Why should the kids have all the fun?"

Volunteering with several urban missions organizations had given the Garricks a taste of working with people of different ethnic backgrounds. When the opportunity arose to join a construction crew in a third-world country for several days, they jumped at the chance. After they returned, they corresponded with the people they'd met, found more volunteers to go the next year, headed a crew the third year, and couldn't wait to go for a fourth year. Once was not enough!

Reflecting back over what they had experienced, Ed said, "The first year I went with my *own* mission—if the last group was able to build *one* house in a week, why, we could build *two*! I managed to borrow a generator, a block cutter, and several other 'modern necessities' that would speed us along. Fortunately, I met with the project director *before* I mentioned my plans to anyone else!

"She told me, 'If we build two houses this week, we'll fail at our *real* mission, which is building community. We want to build with *their* tools so we understand the challenges they face. We want to get to know them and their needs.' As she talked of the transient, despair-filled lives of the townspeople who lived in 'homes' made of cardboard boxes, I began to understand the true nature of our mission.

"We *are* really building a community, not just homes, so that these people can put down roots instead of being drawn to the big cities filled with subsistence jobs and horrid living conditions. Now that the project has built almost two hundred houses, the people themselves have built a church! They've started a store! Those whose houses are already finished can't wait to help build one for their neighbors."

Linda added, "But when we're there, if they have a choice between finishing a house or sitting down to an extra meal with us, they'll choose the meal every time. They place a much higher value on relationships than we do. We fit in best when we leave our watches behind and try to adapt to the pace of their lives, instead of worrying about the task we came to do.

"While we aren't at a point in our lives where we could go overseas on a long-term basis, with the people we've come to know, we feel *connected* on a long-term basis. We can aid in planning how to best meet their needs."

Ed speaks earnestly about spotting new needs and meeting them. "My son joined us last year and the first thing he noticed was the lack of play area in the streets—they were dodging cars in the road to play soccer! So this year we are helping them build a children's center and playing field. Because they know we'll be back, they've grown to trust us *and* they are willing to join with us."

"And we'll hold a summer Bible school for the kids for the first time this year, too," Linda said. "Our hope is to tap into their joy to teach more of the basic Bible stories—but I have a feeling I'll learn more from the kids than they will from me!"

"The town is now a magnet for people who want a more stable home. As they settle, they can't help but learn of the active role that Christ plays in the lives of their new neighbors. As we carry bricks and linger over meals, we know that it is really God at work building their community. We just get to be His hands."

Do you have the spiritual gift of apostleship?

- ☐ I am excited about working in multiple church settings and diverse religious communities.
- ☐ I am interested in how the gospel can be brought to those who have never heard it.
- ☐ I am attracted to new ministries, churches, or settings (such as the inner city) where a whole new approach to evangelism or service is needed.
- ☐ Presenting the gospel to a different culture or in a different language sounds enjoyable.
- ☐ The idea of living or visiting different places excites me.
- ☐ I have often envisioned myself as a missionary.

Suggestions for developing your spiritual gift of apostleship:

1. Begin by taking advantage of the many short-term mission opportunities available today. See if you can thrive in a different culture, local or far away, and minister effectively in that setting.
2. Seek out and interview missionaries or those who have started new ministries. Talk to them about what they consider essen-

tial to the success of their efforts. Read the biographies of famous missionaries.

3. Consider working with a ministry that works to bring new methods, services, or ideas to many churches.

Biblical Example

Paul (Acts 17:16–34)

DISCERNMENT

A person with the gift of discernment is adept at recognizing what is of God and what is not of God.

Biblical Reference: "Now to each one the manifestation of the Spirit is given for the common good . . . to another the ability to distinguish between spirits . . ." (1 Corinthians 12:7, 10).

Kit enjoyed working on the last two retreats so much that she readily volunteered to act as the spiritual director for the next one. She threw herself eagerly into the preparations, chose her themes, and met with her assistant, a young minister named Dale. At their first meeting, Dale said, "I love these retreats—such great opportunities to share how I've been helped." He related several difficulties in his life over the past few years.

Kit was thankful to have a hard-working, enthusiastic partner, but later as she thought about their meeting, she grew uneasy. Dale had talked exclusively about his *past*, saying little about his *faith*. She wondered what role his beliefs had played in his recent crises—he certainly hadn't told her. "Well," she thought, "even if his motives are mixed or his thoughts jumbled right now, it won't necessarily harm the retreat." She decided to pray for guidance as she continued to work with Dale, who at least seemed outwardly sincere.

At the first meeting with the rest of the retreat team, Dale was well received. One woman commented to Kit, "I like his openness.

He readily admits his own shortcomings, and I think the people who come will relate well to his story." However, during a planning discussion for a chapel service, Kit again became uneasy. Dale seemed to steer the discussion. Normally she welcomed unusual ideas for worship, so Kit couldn't quite put her finger on what bothered her about Dale's concept for the chapel service. "Am I somehow jealous of the connections he easily made with the other leaders?" she thought.

A week later, as she reviewed Dale's rough draft for his opening lecture, her feelings came together. The talk was both engaging and touching and would surely capture the attention of the audience. However, while there was nothing out-of-bounds in what Dale said, it fell short of the goals they had set together for this particular talk. Since the purpose of the retreat was to help people experience the grace of God as displayed through Jesus, the lack of anything specifically Christian in Dale's draft was troubling.

Kit gave Dale a call. "I liked the example in your talk of how your friend helped you, but I was wondering about your tie-in to the lecture's scripture verse. There's more here on your personal victory than on how God helped you."

There was a pause. "Well . . . to be truthful, there were times where I didn't think God was being very helpful." What followed was a torrent of doubts over God's role in his life.

Kit thought, *Lord, give me guidance.*

"Dale," she began gently, "God allows us to doubt Him and ask, 'Why?' However, the purpose of this retreat is to let people catch a glimpse of the love God has for them, love so strong that Jesus died for us. The participants have plenty of chances to question, to ponder, to talk with each other and with us alone about what they are hearing. But, Dale, if we leave God's grace out of our teaching, they may as well not come."

They talked for a long time, but Kit knew from the start that even though the retreat was less than a week away, she needed to find another assistant. In the end Dale agreed that he needed more time to heal and work out his own spiritual questions. He asked Kit to let him withdraw from the leadership team.

Could Kit have made her decision about Dale's participation earlier? Sometimes her gift of discernment came through like a herd of elephants, telling her to act then and there. This time, though, her discerning thoughts were less clear. Perhaps God had wanted her to move slowly in the hope that Dale would be swayed to his original love of Jesus by the fellowship of the team. Kit had no way of knowing, but she felt assured that her prayerful consideration of Dale's role had been helped by her gift of discernment.

Do you have the spiritual gift of discernment?

☐ I can generally rely on my first impressions of people and whether their motives or character are authentic. I tend to "know" where a person is coming from.

☐ I sometimes sense when something like a book or presentation will bring people closer to God—or cause them to be pushed away.

☐ In many situations, I find my gut reacting to the circumstance or atmosphere I am experiencing, whether good or bad.

☐ My mind tends to pick up on whether books or speakers are in line with truths as revealed in the Bible. Contradictions stand out for me.

☐ I can distinguish different, nongodly sources of spiritual energy.

Suggestions for developing your spiritual gift of discernment:

1. Consider enrolling in an in-depth Bible study to strengthen your knowledge and understanding of God's truth.

2. Work with others who have this gift to test your discernments. Review church curriculum, participate in book studies, or work through difficult personal issues.

3. Of paramount importance for those with the gift of discernment is understanding the biblical difference between judging to condemn—which is only within God's domain—and judging in a merciful and compassionate way to bring good to the Body of Christ. Some people with this gift find a need to refrain from confrontations until they have grown in Christian maturity. In order to best use discernment, one must work through difficult situations with love, patience, kindness, and understanding.

Biblical Example

Peter and Simon the sorcerer (Acts 8:18–24)

ENCOURAGEMENT/COUNSELING

A person with the gift of encouragement has the ability to effectively listen to people, comforting, encouraging, and assisting them in moving toward psychological and relational wholeness.

Biblical Reference: "We have different gifts, according to the grace given us. If a [person's] gift is . . . encouraging, let him encourage . . ." (Romans 12:6, 8).

Kendra exclaimed, "Whew!" as she set her tray at the last empty spot at the table. "Just in time for an upbeat lunch hour."

"What do you mean?" asked Jamal.

"If *you're* here, Jamal, everyone ends up cheerful," Kendra said as she reached for a napkin. "We forget our problems and talk about things that are 'above' the grapevine or office politics."

"Jamal, I'll never forget my first months here," added Paul. "I was so intimidated by all of the talented advertising experts that I was ready to give up. You encouraged me to draft my brochure idea, which brought in some of my prime accounts. I never would have tried it if you hadn't bugged me about it; I didn't think I could design marketing materials, and look at me now—a group manager!"

"Ditto for me," broke in Kendra. "The rest of you probably don't know that Jamal asked me to do new employee training when I was really just a new employee myself. Remember, Jamal? You saw me demonstrate the new phone system to two of my colleagues who had missed the demonstration. You told my manager that anyone who could teach others to set up their voice mailbox properly could teach company procedures—and I love the work I do in training now."

"And you encouraged me to write up my ideas for the annual

meeting after I vented my frustration to you about the planning session," added Tanya. "They didn't use all of them, of course, but they asked me to head the investor relations committee! I'm having so much fun making this event more meaningful for our stockholders."

Jamal smiled at his friends around the table. "Hey, a bad day is any day that I'm stuck at my desk with no chance to listen to your ideas or frustrations and help you dream about what you *could* be doing."

"Well, I move that we figure out how to get you out of your office a bit more," said Paul. "Your job description should carry the title of 'Official Sounding Board.' I feel that all of my ideas are safe with you: you listen to what I have to say and give credit for the merits of the idea before making suggestions. If that's all you did here, day in and day out, you'd be worth every penny of your salary, given the creative energy we all gain through your encouragement."

Do you have the spiritual gift of encouragement/counseling?

- ☐ People tell me that I am a good listener.
- ☐ Others seem to be comfortable approaching me with their problems.
- ☐ I often see attributes or gifts in others that they are slow to recognize for themselves.
- ☐ I am usually aware of the emotional state of people around me, whether they are content or whether something is bothering them.
- ☐ In stressful situations I often find myself able to give perspective of what is positive in a way that others find helpful.
- ☐ I tend to have more faith in people than they have in themselves.
- ☐ I sympathize easily with others and am tolerant of their shortcomings, yet I enjoy helping people mature in their faith.

Suggestions for developing your spiritual gift of encouragement/counseling:

1. Consider your other spiritual gifts and life gifts and discover how they best work with the spiritual gift of encouragement/counseling. Teachers may work best in smaller groups

where they can be more encouraging. Those with the spiritual gift of mercy might want to seek out areas of service with more individual contact with others.

2. Consider training for one-on-one counseling or lay ministries that emphasize listening to others and walking beside them in times of crisis.

3. Make sure you have your own encouragers to give you strength as you pursue your encourager/counselor role. If you have this spiritual gift, remember that it is easy to become overloaded with the demands of others.

4. Consider being trained as a small group leader, using your gift to make each group meeting a time of encouragement for all.

Biblical Example

Barnabas (Acts 11:23–24)

EVANGELISM

A person with the gift of evangelism has the willingness and ability to spread the Good News of Jesus Christ to those who don't know Him in a way that makes them respond in faith and discipleship.

Biblical Reference: "But to each one of us grace has been given as Christ apportioned it. . . . It was he who gave some to be . . . evangelists . . ." (Ephesians 4:7–11).

Sarah listened carefully to her friend Beth's description of the painful end to yet another romantic relationship. Beth complained, "Why do I always end up on the hurting side of love? This has happened too many times."

Sarah and Beth had known each other all through their school years. While Sarah had never kept her church membership a secret, she seldom had opportunities to discuss her faith at school or with her friends. Now, as she and Beth talked about Beth's need for approval and the void left when her father moved out, Sarah felt a need to take the conversation to a deeper level. "You know, Beth, this romantic void in your life is really just a symptom of the bigger void in your life, that of not knowing Jesus. The more I learn of the unconditional love of Jesus, the less I am hurt by what others do."

Beth looked at her, startled, and said, "No, you're wrong. I don't feel a void like that. "

Sarah wisely went back to her listening mode, but just a few days later, Beth asked her what she meant about Jesus. Sarah told her the story of Jesus in her own words, explaining the differences it made in her own life. Beth asked one or two questions, then changed the subject to the upcoming weekend's events.

A few weeks later Beth called, asking if Sarah would come and meet Kira, a new friend of hers. Together, Kira and Beth challenged Sarah with every spiritual question in the book: If God is so good, why is there pain? What about people who have never heard about Christ? Is the Bible for real? And so on. Sarah carefully and enthusiastically answered each question as fully as she could, knowing that their interest showed a thirst for faith. She had always been interested in these same themes and had prayerfully sought out answers in the past few years. However, Beth was still not ready to believe as Sarah did.

Three months later, Beth called Sarah and excitedly told her about a Christian seminar she had attended. After talking with the speaker at length, Beth had joined a class for those wanting to be baptized. Beth finished, "Thanks so much for your listening ears and for not treating me like a Sunday school project."

Do you have the spiritual gift of evangelism?

- ☐ I enjoy studying questions that challenge Christianity.
- ☐ I frequently think about people who do not have a faith commitment, wishing they could understand how my faith helps me.
- ☐ I look for ways that might help others understand the difference Christianity can make in their lives.
- ☐ I can see how people's needs can be met through Christian faith.
- ☐ I can comfortably talk about my Christian faith with others

in a way that makes them comfortable as well.

☐ I enjoy many friendships outside the faith community.

☐ I get excited about sharing God's Good News with others and am thrilled when they receive the forgiveness of God.

Suggestions for developing your spiritual gift of evangelism:

1. Basic to using the gift of evangelism in any setting is a clear understanding of the Bible's message of forgiveness through Christ and the ability (which may come only through practice) to convey the message in your own style. Talk with others who have this gift about methods they use. Also, there are many books on the subject.
2. Study the areas that block those who are distant from Christ from coming to Him. Become well-informed about how to respond to their questions. There are many workshops and books available to help you in the area of apologetics.
3. Seek out a person on your church staff who either has this gift or can direct you to a person who does so that you can network with him or her.

Biblical Example

Philip (Acts 8:26–38)

FAITH

A person with the gift of faith has the ability to recognize what God wants accomplished as well as sustain a stalwart belief that God will see it done despite what others perceive as barriers.

Biblical Reference: "Now to each one the manifestation of the Spirit is given for the common good ... to another faith by the same

Spirit . . ." (1 Corinthians 12:7, 9).

Sixteen, seventeen, eighteen robes with holes or split seams. . . . This was not a matter of vanity, unrealistic expectations, or dissatisfaction. This was a matter of necessity. Nyssa knew that if the choir robes went through the wash one more time, the holes in those eighteen robes would be visible from the back of the church balcony.

Some people probably thought choir robes were too formal, but other members of Nyssa's church might quit the choir if they had to sit up front with their clothes on display week after week. Robes equalized the wardrobes of the "haves" and the "have nots" in their urban neighborhood. There wasn't enough money to purchase new robes of any quality, nor did she have the ability or time to make new ones. Then a thought came to her—that ministry she had heard of . . .

She dialed the phone. "Yes, is Felice there? Hi, I'm from the Shiloh Community Church. I read an article about the way you help churches sew their own choir robes. Could you explain your program to me?"

Felice was glad to share what she did. "Well, several years ago I happened upon a style of needlework that adapts well to assembly-line sewing and created robes for my church that many others admired. Only a few of the steps required more than basic sewing skills. I enjoyed showing others how to do it, but thought, *Why not turn this into my own little ministry?* I get a wholesale price on the fabrics through a company that believes in what I'm doing. You provide a sewing team that cuts out each of the garments and stitches the basic seams. I smock the tops and finish the corners, then turn the hem work and hooks back to you. I just ask that you make a set not only for your own church but for two other churches that are in need. So far, I've helped twenty churches, with fifty sets shipped to inner-city parishes or overseas—a few groups couldn't stop at three sets but kept going!"

Nyssa thought quickly. There weren't many women in her congregation with time on their hands, but the idea of passing on their gift might be enough of an incentive. . . . "We'll do it. Can we invite you to a meeting to tell us about your work in person?"

Felice went on to explain the number of work hours it would take to make forty robes for themselves, then eighty more. After the phone call, Nyssa added it up, divided it, adjusted it for coffee breaks, and started to pray, "Lord, change my mind quickly if we don't really need choir robes, because once Felice places the fabric order, there's no backing out.

"But if this is right for us, help me find the right prayer partners, the right hands . . . and a couple of serger machines for all of those long seams!"

The choir director thought Nyssa was crazy—hundreds of volunteer hours were needed. Her friends agreed to help but told Nyssa, "We sparse few are going to be sewing for years to meet our obligations—it will be too hard to find others to help!" However, one friend recalled another project that Nyssa had put her shoulder to, and said, "If she says we can do this, maybe we can."

Nyssa called two women in the congregation who made their living as tailors and was delighted to find that they had been eyeing the old robes with thoughts of action as well. With these experienced garment makers at the helm, they had no trouble finding people to commit to starting three robes or more apiece.

Not only that, but "Project Robed in Majesty" turned into a time of spiritual renewal for those who participated. Gathering weekly in a back room of the church where they were able to spread their supplies, they chose to listen to tapes and readings, discussing as they worked.

When the choir at last was clad in the new robes, Nyssa tried to sidestep the role her faith had played, but her example encouraged those around her to step out in faith the next time it was their turn to trust and act.

Do you have the spiritual gift of faith?

☐ I firmly believe God is active in our lives.

☐ Sometimes I sense that God is orchestrating a project or idea. I find it easy to encourage and support it when others have doubts.

☐ I believe deeply in the power of prayer and am aware of God's presence in my life.

☐ I am able to believe that God is faithful, even in the face of seemingly insurmountable difficulties.

☐ People often tell me I am an "incurable optimist."

☐ My personal experiences help me believe in the power of faith.

Suggestions for developing your spiritual gift of faith:

1. Pray with those who have the gift of faith. Talk through your life circumstances with them to see where God has been at work.
2. Study the lives of those with the gift of faith such as George Mueller, a nineteenth-century Christian. Mueller is best known for the orphanages he headed and his commitment to only depend upon prayer for support. A summary of his life can be found in Andrew Murray's *The Believer's School of Prayer* (Bethany House Publishers, 1982).
3. Practice trusting the Lord with small things. As your faith and insight increase, look to God for help in larger arenas where God is at work.

Biblical Example

The centurion (Matthew 8:5–10)

GIVING

A person with the gift of giving is able to give of material wealth freely and with joy to further God's causes.

Biblical Reference: "We have different gifts, according to the grace given us . . . if it is contributing to the needs of others, let [them] give generously . . ." (Romans 12:6, 8).

The question of replacing the old electric organ with a pipe organ had never been raised before, but the company that had serviced it for years declared that the old organ was irreparable. As Lee, the head of the worship committee, looked over the estimated replacement costs, she thought to herself, "Why not a pipe organ now? The new sanctuary was designed to hold one and the estimates are still on file."

As she looked at the significant amount of money a pipe organ cost, a plan began to form in her mind. She thought of people in the congregation who agreed with her that while great music was perhaps not required by God, it definitely helped many worshipers feel closer to their Lord and deepened their worship experiences. She decided that her vacation savings could start off the fund-raising—she'd willingly make do with a week of fun here in town, knowing that her "vacation" was spent on the organ!

With the blessing of the pastoral staff, over the next week she met with eight different couples, outlining the need for a new pipe organ. "I don't want to bring this before the congregation without being sure that the idea is well supported. I hope to find a few individuals who are willing and able to donate enough money to give the organ fund a substantial start. If the rest of our members see that the goal is attainable, perhaps they will want to make contributions they can afford."

Several of the couples decided that they wanted to support the project, provided that their names remained anonymous. Three families agreed to give additional "matching grants" if others in the congregation donated larger sums.

By the time Lee was ready to tell the congregation of the plans for a new organ, about half the money needed had been pledged. She urged, "Pray about whether this is a project you should support. I know that some may say an organ benefits our congregation in a selfish way. We don't want this to detract from the other causes and missions we support. Yet music can enhance our own spiritual lives. We aren't going for the fanciest organ available but believe that we are being wise stewards of what we have."

The church posted a thermometer chart so the incoming pledges could be recorded. One family was able to commit to a large pledge—for their financial situation—by agreeing to make their own pizza on Fridays rather than ordering takeout. A men's prayer group volunteered to do some extensive repair work for the church on condition that the savings be donated to the organ fund. The youth group decided to change their annual ski trip destination to a closer resort, giving the savings to the fund.

Soon, Lee was able to report to the congregation that over ninety percent of the needed money was pledged. "We will have a new organ, but let's stick to our plan of not borrowing funds for this. This is a spiritual adventure of sorts, and we'll have to wait for the last page to discover the ending."

And in the end, Lee received a note from one of the families she had contacted initially. "We knew that God wanted us to contribute to the organ fund, but we waited to see what others could do without us. This check should cover the remainder needed— and may our church continue to raise funds in this God-led way."

Do you have the spiritual gift of giving?

- ☐ I often give generously and joyfully.
- ☐ I like to find ways to free up my resources to benefit others.
- ☐ I feel a sense of ownership in the ministries and projects I support financially.
- ☐ I'd rather give anonymously, for the most part, unless my example might inspire others to be generous.
- ☐ I tend to manage my own money well, often basing financial decisions on what will be made available for giving.
- ☐ I feel comfortable and have success with approaching others to give of their resources.

Suggestions for developing your spiritual gift of giving:

1. Study the Bible's teachings on money and possessions.
2. Network with others who have developed systems for knowing when, where, and how much to give. Research the ministries that interest you in order to discern whether your resources are well used.
3. When others in your family do not have the gift of giving or do not believe in supporting Christian-related outreach, giving can become a source of conflict. Try to involve these individuals in your decision-making process as much as possible. Be sensitive to their needs for financial security. If possible, pray together about giving opportunities and/or look for other ways to give.

Biblical Example

The early Church in Jerusalem (Acts 4:32–35)

HEALING

A person with the gift of healing is able to call on God for the curing of illness and the restoration of health in a supernatural way.

Biblical Reference: "Now to each one the manifestation of the Spirit is given for the common good . . . to another gifts of healing by that one Spirit . . ." (1 Corinthians 12:7, 9).

In *Light in My Darkest Night*[3] Catherine Marshall tells of her personal struggle with the death of her infant granddaughter despite the fervent prayers and efforts of many strong Christians, including sixteen friends who joined them for a four-day prayer retreat. One of these friends, Jamie Buckingham, related how during a prayer session for the baby, he suddenly remembered a letter from a friend who asked for prayers for a little girl who was dying of cystic fibrosis. Jamie realized that the little girl was in the very same hospital. He found her room and stepped into a crazed scene as two nurses worked to restore the child's breathing. He asked if he could pray for her:

> "Lord, heal this child in Jesus' name," I prayed.
>
> It was brief. Just a few sentences, then I withdrew my hand and was gone. It was not until after I returned to my home in Melbourne, Florida, more than a week later that I got the news. . . . A miracle had happened, [my friend] reported. Remember the little girl with cystic fibrosis who had been dying in the Boston hospital? Well, she had just been released, allowed to go home. The doctors said they must have made a mistake. It wasn't cystic fibrosis after all—because that's incurable. And the child was fine now. Healed completely.

This is the enigma of the gift of healing in the Church today: though both were blanketed in prayer, the Marshall baby died and

---

[3]Catherine Marshall, *Light in My Darkest Night* (Old Tappan, N.J.: Fleming H. Revell Company, 1989), p. 104.

the other young girl lived. Jamie Buckingham might have denied that he had the gift of healing, having witnessed few miracles and many deaths. Some say that the gift of healing was more widespread during apostolic times as God's way of strengthening faith, but the same questions arose then. Paul clearly had the gift, as he showed during his stay on Malta:

> There was an estate nearby that belonged to Publius, the chief official of the island. He welcomed us to his home and for three days entertained us hospitably. His father was sick in bed, suffering from fever and dysentery. Paul went in to see him and, after prayer, placed his hands on him and healed him. When this had happened, the rest of the sick on the island came and were cured. (Acts 28:7–9)

Yet we read in Philippians 2:25–27 that Paul's close friend Epaphroditus was very sick and nearly died. Trophimus, another friend of Paul's, had to be left behind at Miletus because of illness (2 Timothy 4:20). Apparently Paul could not heal all those who were very ill, and clearly the gift of healing does not function at all times.

There is little direct instruction about healing in the New Testament. While Jesus models a vibrant healing ministry for us, much is left as a mystery. Healing is best understood as just one more way God shows us His love. When healing is elevated above other spiritual gifts, God's love can get lost in the distraction. Those who are not healed may feel that God disapproves of them. A healing ministry can remain authentic by staying biblical, focusing on God as the healer, rather than on those who are doing the praying.

People with the true gift of healing are without exception good listeners. They listen to God, following inner leadings on when to speak, when to stay silent, and how to pray. They listen to the sick, discerning the root causes of illness, whether physical, emotional, relational, or spiritual. They listen to the needs of those who are ill. Occasionally the sick have heard too many healing prayers; they just want to talk to a friend.

Those with the gift of healing operate out of compassion and view their healing prayers as acts of humble obedience to God. Rather than seeing healing prayer as something to attain, they see it as a normal part of the Christian life. They pray with confidence, believing that God can heal and that prayer can overcome any evil influences hindering a person. They also pray honestly, making sure that those they pray for understand that not all are healed and that the whys and wherefores are truly a mystery.

Do you have the spiritual gift of healing?

- [ ] I am naturally drawn to those who are sick either in spirit or in body.
- [ ] Sometimes God seems to work through my prayers to bring physical, spiritual, relational, or emotional healing to others.
- [ ] I am aware of God's presence and try to follow His guidance for how to pray in each situation where healing is desired.
- [ ] Often I can sense whether a person's problems are physical or emotional in origin.
- [ ] When petitions for healing are spoken, I find myself wanting to pray.

Suggestions for developing your spiritual gift of healing:

1. To hold yourself accountable for using this gift for God's purposes, make sure that you have mature Christian friends or associates.
2. Begin to seek out people who are already using this gift. Observe their methods.
3. As a source of encouragement for yourself, journal or record the places where God is moving and healing.
4. Do not become discouraged if people aren't healed the first time you pray. Sometimes multiple prayers result in healing; sometimes God has another agenda.

HELPS

A person with the gift of helps has the ability to work alongside others and attaches spiritual value to the accomplishment of practical and often behind-the-scenes tasks that sustain the Body of Christ.

Biblical Reference: "*And in the church God has appointed . . . those able to help others . . .*" *(1 Corinthians 12:28).*

Chandra frequently spoke at women's luncheons and was thus expecting the usual church-basement atmosphere for her presentation. She could therefore not have been more surprised to find the fellowship hall of this small church glistening with a festive atmosphere that almost took her breath away. As she examined the "starlit" ceiling more closely, she realized that the effect had been achieved with black paper, small lights, and lots of cheesecloth. In the far corner, two people were up on ladders, taping the few last decorations into place.

Chandra walked over to the man and woman to introduce herself. She said, "I don't think I've ever spoken in such a beautiful room. How did you dream up such lovely decorations?"

"They weren't *my* idea," Tom answered. "All I did was show up about an hour ago and make myself available for whatever needed to be done."

"That's all you ever do," commented Ellen, the woman on the other ladder, as she reached for the next light, "and ten minutes after you show up, things start getting done! The decorations may have been my idea, but we'd be eating this dinner on paper place mats under fluorescent lights without your assistance, Tom!"

"I just help with what needs to be done."

"That's an interesting way to put it," said Chandra. "You know, God uses the word 'helper' to describe Eve in the book of Genesis. The only other times it is used are once to describe King David and *sixteen times* to describe *God* as the source of strong, powerful help. I wouldn't be here tonight if someone at the foundation where I work hadn't helped with my travel arrangements, taken care of our correspondence, and prepared the handouts. I have no idea why I have a gift for teaching and you have a gift for helping, but this wouldn't be much of an evening if either one of us were missing. Helping is much more important than most people think."

Ellen spoke again. "I've always known that to be true. You know, I love helping with the costuming for our annual children's program, but don't ask me to lead the rehearsals. And I love helping with fund-raising for our mission teams. I believe so strongly in what they are doing, but I don't think I'd make a very good missionary. It feels right, though, to be a part of their work in a different way. Helping others is my way of passing along some of the love that God has given to me."

Tom added, "To me, it doesn't matter what I do. I can celebrate the ways that God operates through whatever team I'm on, whatever role I play."

Do you have the spiritual gift of helps?

- [ ] I tend to notice and assist with practical tasks that need to be done.
- [ ] As I do routine tasks, I feel a spiritual link to the ministries or people I serve.
- [ ] I would rather be responsible for set tasks than be involved in leadership.
- [ ] I prefer to work behind the scenes and often avoid public recognition for what I do.
- [ ] I receive satisfaction through quietly serving others.
- [ ] I enjoy working on odd jobs, often seeing a need and tending to it without being asked.

Suggestions for developing your spiritual gift of helps:

1. Remember that the gift of helps furthers God's kingdom. The tasks helpers do are an important work that God values highly!
2. Talk with people who share your passions or interests but have different gifts and discover where you can help them. Leaders, evangelists, teachers, shepherds, etc., all need help.
3. When you work with others, speak up about what has to

happen. Not everyone spots ways to help as easily as you do!

Biblical Example

Administrators in the early Church (Acts 6:1–7)

HOSPITALITY

A person with the gift of hospitality provides a warm welcome for people that demonstrates God's love by providing food, shelter, or fellowship.

Biblical Reference: "Be hospitable to one another without complaining. Like good stewards of the manifold grace of God, serve one another with whatever gift each of you has received" (1 Peter 4:9–10, NRSV).

Take yourself back to the 1970s when most people still dressed up for church, even for committee meetings. For a certain suburban congregation, the attire of many in the very active youth group had become an issue. With a worried expression, the pastor told the teen leaders, "You wouldn't believe the number of phone calls I get from members who assume that clothes reveal a person's attitude toward worship! I know we should welcome the teenagers no matter what they wear, but this issue is splitting the congregation. Either they stop wearing jeans or they stop meeting here."

Ben, one of the youth leaders, leaned over to talk to his wife, Trish. Nodding, she spoke up. "There are things happening with the teens that are more important than what they wear. I understand your dilemma, but we have a different solution. We'll meet at our house. They can come in chains and leather, as far as I'm concerned, so long as they bring their Bibles and continue to grow in their faith."

The others looked at Ben and Trish in surprise. Attendance at the Sunday teen Bible study averaged seventy-five people, several

94

guitars, and a lot of food. In their house? Ben added, "They can come Wednesday nights, too. *We* will welcome them until the church agrees on how to do the same."

And welcome them they did. The teen leaders soon began coming a bit early to help push back the furniture, pop the popcorn, and pour the beverages. The young people were astounded at the warmth of the hospitality shown to them. When one boy asked why they did it, Ben replied, "No matter who we are entertaining, we like to challenge ourselves—can we make our guests as welcome as we would want Jesus to feel if He were our visitor today?"

Trish added, "We found long ago that our attitude matters the most. If we hustle and bustle to serve the finest hors d'oeuvres, our guests may feel our anxiety and be uncomfortable. Better to serve takeout chicken by a lighted fire and enjoy their conversation, if that's what helps us relax and enjoy our guests."

Ben continued, "Everyone deserves the feeling that they are important to others. That's why we wanted to have all of you gather here. We have the privilege of seeing you learn and grow spiritually. What other reward do we need?"

Ben and Trish hosted the teens for a little over two years. In that time, the congregation grew to recognize the powerful impact that this ministry was having on the young people. Eventually, the meetings returned to the church building. Years later, though, Ben and Trish continue to receive letters and calls from those teens, thanking them for the role the couple played in their faith journeys. What other reward could they need?

Do you have the spiritual gift of hospitality?

- ☐ I am comfortable around strangers and care deeply about how my church welcomes them.
- ☐ I can make all kinds of people feel welcome.
- ☐ I enjoy providing a safe environment for those in need.
- ☐ I feel fulfilled when I can open my home to others for food and fellowship.
- ☐ I am more concerned with whether guests feel welcome than whether my house is in order.
- ☐ I love to create appealing and appropriate environments for people.
- ☐ I view relationships as opportunities to pass on God's love.

Suggestions for developing your spiritual gift of hospitality:

1. Step out in faith! Even if your dining room isn't big enough or your budget doesn't allow for shrimp, you will find that God blesses card tables, hot dishes, and potlucks. As you try different ways of entertaining, be aware of how you approach the events. Monitor your worry. Know that you can pick and choose how you will demonstrate hospitality. Not everyone needs to host crowds.
2. Study the importance of true simplicity and how it can set you free to concentrate on the people you are serving rather than on the preparations and details of showing hospitality.
3. Find out who works with visitors or congregational care at your church. Partner with those people. Make it a point every Sunday to meet someone new. Realize that almost every ministry in the church needs to offer a Christlike atmosphere. As Jesus said, "But when you give a banquet, invite the poor, the crippled, the lame, the blind, and you will be blessed. Although they cannot repay you, you will be repaid at the resurrection of the righteous" (Luke 14:13–14).

Biblical Example

Lydia (Acts 16:13–15)

KNOWLEDGE

A person with the gift of knowledge has the ability to understand, organize, and effectively use information, from either natural sources or the Holy Spirit directly, for the advancement of God's purposes.

Biblical Reference: "Now to each one the manifestation of the Spirit is given for the common good. To one there is given . . . the message of knowledge by means of the same Spirit" (1 Corinthians 12:7–8).

At the previous meeting of the missions committee, the general consensus was this: "We have to find a project close to home that will fire the imaginations of the congregation. Most of our members can't afford to travel or take a week off of work, but many say they want to be involved in a hands-on outreach." When Vicki volunteered to check into some possibilities, no one on the committee expected the kind of report she gave the next week.

"As we discussed last time," Vicki began, "whatever project we choose needs to be within an hour's drive of here. We also said that based on past efforts, most of our members prefer ministries where multiple types of talents are needed—not just a building project, for example, but a building project where people from our church are also needed for educational efforts, child care, meal preparation, or some other combination, so that all family members can participate.

"With these criteria in mind, I called several other churches and foundations in the area and identified seven alternatives. I also talked to each of the project heads to establish if the Christian faith was compatible with their efforts, therefore providing a match for us." Vicki handed out charts that showed each project, the ideal number of volunteers, cost to the church, location, and almost anything else they needed to know. Attached to every chart was a page for each of the different outreaches, describing in detail their goals and needs.

One of the committee members asked, "Which project do you believe would be best?"

Vicki said earnestly, "I haven't analyzed it yet—I just wanted you to have all the information necessary for us to make a good decision. Are there any questions?"

With the information so well gathered and presented, the members adjourned, agreeing to pray about the alternatives before their next time together.

The committee leader began the next meeting by asking for input on Vicki's seven alternatives. Bill spoke first. "While all of the choices have merit, I found myself drawn to the second. As I prayed about this outreach, I saw an image of the teens from our church building a bridge with the teens at this crisis center. If this is the project we choose, my impression is that our youth would be the main connection through which the rest of us are able to serve. Whether that is our goal or not I can't answer, but the thought of a project that excites the teenagers of our church is powerful to me."

"There *are* a lot of teens at that center on a regular basis," Vicki added. "Your insight may be right on target, Bill."

Note that while Vicki's gift of knowledge here operated in a natural way, Bill's gift of knowledge operated in a supernatural way—Vicki's report had mentioned nothing about the teens. Both gifts of knowledge guided the committee's decision.

Do you have the spiritual gift of knowledge?

- ☐ It is easy for me to gather and analyze information for projects, ministries, or other causes within the Body of Christ.
- ☐ I enjoy studying the Bible and other books to gain insights and background for God's Word.
- ☐ I can organize information well to pass on to others.
- ☐ I seem to understand how God acts in our lives.
- ☐ At times I find myself knowing information about a situation that has not been told to me by anyone else.

Suggestions for developing your spiritual gift of knowledge:

1. Consider enrolling in an in-depth Bible study. Knowledge of Scripture will enhance your understanding of any other projects you undertake.
2. List the areas in which you already have a vast knowledge base and other areas where you have a passion to learn more. Talk to leaders at your church about where your gift of knowledge can be used.
3. Volunteer to research the information needed for an upcoming outreach or project. Work with someone who has done this in the past.
4 If you find yourself having hunches or trains of thought that seem to be giving you information, write them down or talk them out. This will allow you to ponder later what the information might mean. Always test your hunches against Scripture!

Biblical Example

Luke, the author of Luke and Acts

Note:

Knowing the difference between gifts of *prophecy, knowledge,* and *wisdom* can often be confusing. To clarify:

Prophecy generally means declaring from God's perspective what is right or wrong in a given circumstance, perhaps indicating the future consequences of continuing on the present path.

Knowledge is generally factual information about people or a situation that can be useful and insightful for making decisions.

Wisdom is generally a *clarifying* insight that cuts to the core of a paradox or conflict, identifying the solution or exposing the deeper dynamics of an issue.

LEADERSHIP

A person with the gift of leadership has the ability to motivate, coordinate, and direct the efforts of others in doing God's work.

Biblical Reference: "We have different gifts, according to the grace given us . . . if it is leadership, let him govern diligently . . ." (Romans 12:6, 8).

A true leader knows when a task is too great for one person to handle, but true leaders don't get people to work *for* them. They get people to work together *with* them toward a common goal. Excellence in leadership happens when one person convinces two or three others to work on the same common goal, surrounding him or herself with dedicated, knowledgeable people who perform their tasks in a consistently superior, coordinated manner.

For Joel, leadership happened when his young daughter asked, "Daddy, I want to do something really special with you—can we go camping again?" Given that it was wintertime in Minnesota, Joel thought long and hard before replying. "Let me see what I can do," he said.

Joel called a few of the other fathers in his men's prayer group. "What if we held a camp-in at church—a fun time to be with our kids, play games, and have snacks. We could really have some great 'quality' time in the midst of the Minnesota deep freeze."

His friends willingly joined in the planning, keeping the details simple so that everyone could have a good time. During the camp-in, Joel saw delight on so many faces that he began to wonder, "What if I could get fathers this excited about parenting more of the time? So many of the dads I know didn't have good role models in their own fathers—they were too busy or too distant."

In the weeks that followed, Joel contacted some friends he thought might share his passion for becoming better fathers. Together they brainstormed about what they might do. They made a proposal to their pastor that the next men's retreat have fatherhood as the theme and volunteered to organize the event.

The retreat proved to be a source of encouragement and inspiration to those who attended. On the second night Joel stood to speak. "I've heard many of you say that this experience has opened your eyes to how much you have to learn about being the kind of father God intended you to be. I know that's been true for me! Who would like to continue meeting so that we can work on these ideas together?"

About a dozen men signed up at the retreat, but as they talked to their friends about what they had learned, more fathers in the church became interested. Joel recruited two of the retreat participants to co-lead with him in planning the direction of the group.

That spring on Fathers' Day, Joel announced a new small group ministry—Down-to-Earth Fathering—to the congregation. "We'll meet once a week before work for fellowship, teaching, and a chance to share our struggles as earthly fathers trying to live up to the example set by our heavenly Father. Of course, none of us can be perfect, but we can be more intentional. We can change the less healthy patterns of how we parent for better ones in order to touch the lives of our children."

The group grew quickly to more than thirty men at each meeting. Joel encouraged others to take on various organizational and teaching roles. As he and another father discussed an upcoming fishing event, the other remarked, "Because of your efforts with this ministry, I've had a chance to be a kid again—in fact, it's even better than that, because my Dad *never* did these kinds of things for me. I am so grateful that I've discovered more joy in being a father."

Do you have the spiritual gift of leadership?

- [ ] I can motivate others and get people to work together toward a common goal.
- [ ] I have enough confidence in my vision of what should be done to give direction to others.
- [ ] I frequently accept responsibility in group settings where leadership is required.
- [ ] People under my leadership sense that they are headed in a good direction.
- [ ] When necessary, I can make unpopular decisions and work through the disagreements that follow.
- [ ] I can see in advance what people can achieve.

Suggestions for developing your spiritual gift of leadership:

1. The Bible has much to say about the servant role of a leader. Anyone possessing this gift should meditate on the passages of Scripture that describe God's perspectives on power, submission, and accountability. A good topical Bible will help in this.
2. Study the methods of those you consider to be great leaders in the eyes of God.
3. Leaders need the support of other visionaries as a check and balance that they are following God's path. Many find it helpful to join a small group for prayer, study, and accountability so that they have a base for discernment.
4. Seek out those with the gifts of wisdom, knowledge, faith, administration, discernment, and perhaps prophecy for guidance.

Biblical Example

Joshua (Joshua 1:1–9)

MERCY

A person with the gift of mercy is able to perceive the suffering of others and comfort and minister effectively with empathy.

Biblical Reference: "We have different gifts, according to the grace given us . . . if it is showing mercy, let [us] do it cheerfully" (Romans 12:6, 8).

Steve knew he needed an extra helping of prayer before his morning's scheduled visit. "God, you know I have no answers for this young family. We have prayed so hard for their little boy to be healed, and we struggle so with his pain. Please let me show your love to them today, and give us your peace. Amen."

Through years of experience, Steve knew that God would help him come alongside others during times of grief and loss. He had long since given up searching for the right things to say, instead concentrating on prayer to help him show God's love in some way. But this visit he knew would be especially tough. The doctors held little hope that young Alex's cancer could be brought under control, and the boy's mother had called Steve, a frequent visitor, to let him know that Alex was having a bad day.

Not quite knowing why, Steve tucked a couple of squirt guns in his pocket. When he arrived, Alex was lying down as he had been all morning. Steve started to sit down beside him, then instead handed him one of the little pistols. "Do you want to have a water fight?"

Alex sat up, his eyes alight for the first time in days. "Do you have two of those? Let's go outside!"

Out they went onto the deck, squirting each other, watering the flowers, and ambushing insects. The morning flew by as Alex reveled in the gift Steve had brought: not only the toys, but the relief of forgetting for a few fun hours that he was so sick.

What seemed like a simple gesture opened the door to heartache for Steve. The joyful play with Alex increased his love for the little boy. Steve's grief was heightened when Alex eventually died, but his gift of mercy afforded Alex much love and support in his short stay on earth. As it is with many gifts, the impact can be subtle and complex. Steve's gift of mercy clearly helped him minister in ways that were beyond what he could do on his own.

Do you have the spiritual gift of mercy?

☐ I get upset when people are hurt, displaced, or rejected, and I want to reach out to them in their suffering.

☐ I enjoy finding ways to show others how much God loves them.

☐ I can frequently see how to comfort people and meet their needs.

☐ I can readily gain the confidence of those in need.

☐ I am able to empathize with hurting people and enter into their healing process.

☐ I tend to see each person as a life that matters to God and reach out to people who are avoided by others.

☐ I enjoy conveying the grace of God to those who feel guilt or shame.

Suggestions for developing your spiritual gift of mercy:

1. Ask to be mentored by those who have the gift of mercy. To build your confidence, go with others to pray and minister to those in need.

2. Pray for God to show you how to be tender and merciful. In many situations, there are no right things to say or do. Memorize Scripture verses that have to do with topics like forgiveness.

3. Using the gift of mercy can be physically and emotionally draining. Beware of overextending yourself. Realize that you may need help from people with other gifts—administration, counseling, or encouragement—as you work with needy people.

4. Setting boundaries is important if you have the gift of mercy. Work to help people to function on their own and become independent once again. Remember, it is *not* merciful to allow people to become too dependent on your help. They need to develop the ability to face important issues in their lives.

Biblical Example

Jesus and the woman of Samaria (John 4: 1–30)

MIRACLES

A person with the gift of miracles can call on God to do supernatural acts that glorify Him.

Biblical Reference: "Now to each one the manifestation of the Spirit is given for the common good. To one there is given through the Spirit . . . miraculous powers . . ." (1 Corinthians 12:7–8, 10).

During one of several periods of intense persecution in the early Church, King Herod executed the apostle James. When Herod saw how pleased the public was with this action, he then arrested Peter. While the Church prayed earnestly, Peter remained in prison until the night before his trial. That night, however, as Peter lay chained to two guards, an angel appeared and awoke Peter as the shackles fell from his wrists:

> Then the angel said to him, "Put on your clothes and sandals." And Peter did so. "Wrap your cloak around you and follow me," the angel told him. Peter followed him out of the prison, but he had no idea that what the angel was doing was really happening; he thought he was seeing a vision. They passed the first and second guards and came to the iron gate leading to the city. It opened for them by itself, and they went through it. When they had walked the length of one street, suddenly the angel left him.

Then Peter came to himself and said, "Now I know without a doubt that the Lord sent his angel and rescued me from Herod's clutches and from everything the Jewish people were anticipating." (Acts 12:8–11)

When Peter made his way to where the believers were gathered, they were sure they were seeing a ghost! It took them a moment to recognize that God had answered their prayers for a miracle. The book of Acts is filled with accounts of miracles that gave authority to the testimony of the apostles as they spread the gospel. We see demons driven out (Acts 16:16–18), no ill effects from a snake bite (Acts 28:1–6), people being raised from the dead (Acts 9:36–42), and more.

By definition, a miracle is an act or event contrary to natural laws, exhibiting God's power over disease, demons, nature, matter, or life itself. People with this gift recognize that their prayers are sometimes answered in ways that defy explanation. Many also have a strong gift of faith and therefore wait confidently for God to act. They are convinced of their own powerlessness apart from God. Rather than specify how God should act to deliver them or others from a situation or what kind of miracle He should perform, those with the spiritual gift of miracles simply pray, as did the early Church during Peter's imprisonment.

Do miracles still happen? What appears as a miracle to some will be explained as coincidence by others. However, some people's lives are filled with so many of these "coincidences" that the term *miracle* begins to be appropriate.

Corrie ten Boom was imprisoned in a Nazi concentration camp for her work in hiding Jewish people.[4] Both she and her sister Betsie were in their mid-fifties at the time of their arrest, not at all prepared to withstand the horrors of prison life. In defiance of their circumstances they used every opportunity to help others and share their faith.

Bibles, of course, were forbidden. Corrie hid hers inside her thin cotton dress as the guards searched them during their arrival at Ravensbruck. The woman in front of her was frisked three times, Betsie and everyone behind her were searched thoroughly. Corrie was never touched. Her Bible was used for study and wor-

---

[4]*The Hiding Place*, by Corrie ten Boom with John and Elisabeth Sherrill. Chosen Books, Inc., Chappaqua, New York, 1971.

ship services in the barracks. So many of the prisoners wanted to participate that they held two gatherings each day.

Then there was the matter of the vitamins. Corrie managed to smuggle in a small sample-size bottle of vitamins for Betsie, who was ill. Betsie refused to hoard it for herself, sharing the precious drops with two dozen other women every day. Even with so many partaking, every time Corrie tipped the bottle another drop appeared. Then one day a friendly guard slipped them a sack full of vitamins, enough for all. Ever practical, Corrie decided that before they touched the new supply, they would finish the bottled drops first. She was unable to coax even one more drop from the bottle. It was completely empty!

After her release, Corrie founded a ministry to ex-prisoners and war victims, including the Nazis who had caused so many to suffer. In 1959, she returned to Ravensbruck to honor her sister and the other 96,000 women who had died there. Only then did she learn that her release was the result of a clerical "error." Just a few days after she was freed, all of the women her age had been sent to the gas chamber.

While some would dismiss these incidents as coincidences, these types of events characterized Corrie's life. In the midst of circumstances as trying as those faced by the early Church, Corrie prayed and saw her prayers answered in mysterious ways time after time.

Today there is evidence that miracles are still occurring on mission frontiers all over the world, authenticating the gospel in the same way the miracles performed by the apostles did in the early Church. At times these miracles display God's power in contrast to that of the local gods—and they lead whole communities to faith in the same way as miracles did in the book of Acts. Others testify of miracles happening regularly in their own congregations in the United States.

Still others believe that we focus too much on visible miracles such as the ones Jesus performed. We neglect the many inner healings, relational healings, and conversions brought about by prayer. Viewed in this light, the gift of miracles clearly still operates every day. Jesus pointed to this when he healed the lame man lowered through the roof. "Which is easier: to say to the paralytic, 'Your sins are forgiven,' or to say, 'Get up, take your mat and walk'? But that you may know that the Son of Man has authority on earth to forgive sins. . . ." He said to the paralytic, "I tell you, get up, take your mat and go home" (Mark 2:9–11). Jesus used the external miracle to authenticate the internal miracle—the kind of miracle that can last an eternity.

Do you have the spiritual gift of miracles?

☐ I find myself praying for things that are obviously beyond the natural capacity of people.

☐ I seek for God to be glorified however my prayers are answered.

☐ I have seen God perform supernatural acts when I have prayed for intervention.

☐ I have seen others accept the Christian faith through these displays of the impossible being accomplished.

☐ I have faith that miracles happen even today.

Suggestions for developing your spiritual gift of miracles:

1. If you believe that miracles is one of your spiritual gifts, become involved in a small group of Christians who are mature in their faith and willing to hold you accountable as you minister to others with this gift.
2. Study clearly the role of miracles in the Bible. Understand God's purposes in allowing miracles to occur.
3. Fellowship with others who also have the gift of miracles.
4. Keep a journal of prayer requests and how they are answered. While moving mountains may be difficult, those who record prayer in this way often see a pattern of miracles at work: their answered prayers become larger and larger in scope.

PASTORING/SHEPHERDING

A person with the gift of shepherding is able to guide and care for other Christians as they experience spiritual growth.

Biblical Reference: "But to each one of us grace has been given as Christ apportioned it. . . . It was he who gave some to be . . . pastors . . ." (Ephesians 4:7, 11).

As the service ended and people began to greet one another, Nick looked around the sanctuary. Sure enough, Bob Rodriguez was once again trying to get his wife out the door as soon as possible, even as she tried to visit with a friend. And there was Lou Stafford, staring at his feet, looking like he'd rather be anywhere else. Nick spotted a couple of other businessmen he knew who didn't seem to be finding "kindred spirits," people to whom they could relate and with whom they could grow spiritually.

Nick often seemed to sense a person's spiritual needs. As he made his way over to Lou, he recalled his own first Sundays at this church, feeling like he was the only one who couldn't find the Scripture passage for the morning's lesson. "Hi, Lou," he began. "I saw you here last week, but you disappeared so fast that I couldn't get over to talk to you. Found anyone you know?"

Lou, glad to see a friendly face, brightened and replied, "Well, Cheryl met some women at the young mothers' group and says this feels like home already. Not that it matters much to me where we go—just so the kids get exposed to some basic religion."

Nick smiled. "Seems like churches tend to make it easier for the women to connect with each other than the men, doesn't it? You know, for a long time I've wanted to get together with some other dads from here. I'm down by your office every Tuesday. What would you think of lunching together, maybe along with Bob Rodriguez and some others? It wouldn't be anything formal, just a chance to meet with other men who are trying to be superdads and super corporate employees as well."

"I'm pretty busy," Lou began, "but we could at least meet once for lunch. How about next week? I see Bob all the time, so I'll check with him."

Over the next few days, Nick managed to find three other fathers to join them for lunch, provided it was "a business lunch and not some religious discussion." Nick carefully planned the first meeting so that no one would feel threatened. He asked everyone to commit to keeping job-related conversation to a minimum. "Once we know what each other does, let's keep work problems at the office and save this time together to talk about the home part of our lives."

The first meeting proved to be a refreshing change of pace for all of them, and they agreed to continue meeting biweekly for the rest of the spring. A month or so later, they began reading together a secular book on values. Soon their discussions took a deeper turn.

After one of the meetings, Lou asked Nick if the two of them could talk a bit longer. "Nick, does this church thing really help you live out this stuff?" Nick took the time to tell Lou how his faith had helped him.

Lou said, "Bob and I have both been thinking of attending the new members' class. These lunches have helped us feel more welcome at church. They've given us more familiar faces—and to be honest, I've realized that my kids aren't the only ones in the family who need to know God. Thanks for including me."

"It's funny," Nick replied, "but I think sometimes God shows me how to band people together. I know I grow more when I meet with the same people for a long period of time, so I enjoy providing these opportunities. If you ever want to help me start another group, give me a call."

"I just might. Thanks."

Gradually several members of the lunch group became active Christians. Each of them acknowledged that Nick had created a place where they could openly raise questions about Christianity. Their frank discussions helped many of them take their spiritual life seriously for the first time in their lives.

Do you have the spiritual gift of shepherding?

- ☐ I enjoy encouraging others to develop in their faith.
- ☐ I tend to think in terms of groups, teams, and task forces

rather than individual personalities as I think about how I might help others.

☐ I have compassion for those who seem to be getting off track. I long to see them come back to the fold.

☐ I would enjoy nurturing and caring for a group of people over a period of time.

☐ I like to see people form long-term, in-depth spiritual relationships.

☐ I can often assess where a person is spiritually; I try to create or look for places where they can connect to enable them to take the next step.

Suggestions for developing your spiritual gift of shepherding:

1. Learn about small group ministry and consider taking small group leadership training.
2. Study how Jesus shepherded His disciples—one of the most diverse small groups ever assembled.
3. Consider working in the recruitment and placement side of the church. Become active in assisting people to connect with or relate to others.
4. To help you guard against fatigue or imbalance in your personal life, be careful to have your own shepherd, perhaps someone with related gifts such as encouragement or teaching.

Biblical Example

Jesus and His disciples

PROPHECY

A person with the gift of prophecy is able to proclaim God's truths in a way relevant to current situations and to envision how God would will things to change.

Biblical Reference: "But to each one of us grace has been given as Christ apportioned it. . . . It was he who gave some to be . . . prophets . . ." (Ephesians 4:7, 11).

Marta found that the more she listened to God, the more God had to tell her—not necessarily about major concerns but about the people around her. She took joy in considering what God might be doing in the life of a friend or colleague. Sometimes she kept the information to herself, but sometimes she felt guided to share it with the person. More and more, she found herself listening to others with one ear on what the person was saying and the other ear tuned to God for what He might have her say to that person.

If this sounds strange, think of how often Jesus used common, everyday things such as bread, coins, water, and lost lambs to speak of spiritual needs to people He met.

One morning as Marta headed out for her daily run, she felt an urge to stop and visit with her neighbor, Lin, who was planting flower bulbs and trying to keep her toddler out of the dirt. As Marta greeted her, Lin said, "The sunshine begged me to come out and tend to the garden, but look at Troy—I'll spend the rest of the day getting the grass stains out of his romper. There's no getting ahead these days!"

Marta sensed God's desire for her to speak to Lin. She reset her stopwatch and knelt down. "Believe me, I remember those days when both my girls were in diapers—the phone ringing just as one or the other was finding a new way to injure herself or break something. But now, they dress themselves, pick up their own messes, and even help me clean the house!"

As she spoke, Marta saw an image of the garden in full bloom and immediately knew what God wanted her to say. "You know, this season of your life is just like the season of your garden. You won't see the results of those bulbs until next spring. Come January, even the planting will seem like a dream! But the flowers will bloom—just as your children will bloom because of the ways you are nurturing them."

Lin looked at her. "That's a great image for me. I love this part of gardening because of its promises. If I take the right steps, the flowers will be fun to see in the springtime. From now on when I look at Troy, I'll imagine him to be a hyacinth. . . . I'll watch for the signs of blossoming.

"You know," Lin added, "coming from someone else, what you said would sound corny, but I know you really mean it. Thanks."

Do you have the spiritual gift of prophecy?

- ☐ I often spot the differences between cultural trends and biblical truths.
- ☐ I tend to see or think of images that convey God's truth.
- ☐ To me, repentance, change, and challenge are a healthy part of our spiritual life. I am very aware of the future consequences of choosing one path or another.
- ☐ I listen carefully to God for what He wants me to say to others.
- ☐ When necessary, I am able to confront people with the truth of a situation.
- ☐ It saddens me when others ignore or take lightly life's problems.
- ☐ Often I can verbalize God's truths in situations where that truth is encouraging—or even where that truth is unpopular or difficult for listeners to accept.

Suggestions for developing your spiritual gift of prophecy:

1. Spend time improving your understanding of biblical standards, the roles and messages of biblical prophets, and the difference between biblical absolutes and relative standards (to avoid, for example, proclaiming that all women today need to cover their heads in church, as Paul directs in 1 Corinthians 11:5).
2. Sometimes believers with the gift of prophecy have difficulty

in leadership roles because of their tendency to use the gift judgmentally. If that is the case for you, make sure you network with people with the spiritual gifts of discernment and wisdom so you have a way to test your prophetic revelations.

3. If you receive hunches, visions, or images, have a notebook nearby so that you can record them and how you are led to interpret them. Again, test what you receive with Scripture and the understanding of mature Christians.

4. Be aware that receiving a prophecy from God and being called to deliver it are two different events. Ask God when, how, and to whom the prophecy is to be given.

Biblical Example

John (Revelation 2)

TEACHING

A person with the gift of teaching has the ability to understand and communicate God's truths to others effectively—in ways that lead to applications in their lives.

Biblical Reference: "We have gifts that differ according to the grace given us: . . . the teacher, in teaching . . ." (Romans 12:6–7, NRSV).

Over their usual cup of coffee after the evening Bible study, Phil asked his friends what they thought of the lesson that night. Did they follow it?

"Grant is such a nice guy, and I'm grateful that he agreed to teach all month," Karen said, "but the study guide is a lifesaver, given the way his teaching jumps around."

"I found myself wondering how the class would go if he stuck to just a couple of points and maybe let us take on some of the questions in small groups," Phil mused. "The whole passage could be better applied to our lives, too. It reminded me of a news story

I read today," and Phil went on to describe the connections he saw.

Rachel broke in, "You should teach the class."

Phil shook his head. "I'm too new to all of this, so new that I feel foolish criticizing Grant after all of the work he puts into the lessons. When I listen to him, though, I find myself thinking of other ways to get the message across."

Ted spoke up. "Why don't you give it a try, Phil? Pick a lesson and share it with us. We'll be kind to you! And, we'll give Grant a call. I'd bet he'd enjoy a breather."

Phil went to the library to prepare and surrounded himself with books on the topic his friends had suggested he teach. When he finally paused to look at his watch, he couldn't believe that two hours had passed; he had been so engrossed in the subject. He was eager to share what he had learned, but was still unsure of the approach to take. What would really drive the message home? Suddenly he thought of a clip from a movie he had seen a few months before. "If I use that as an introduction, then let them talk about the characters with whom they can identify; it will lead right to my main point," he decided. "Whatever made me think of that?"

At the next meeting, watching his friends become as excited over the material as he was, he realized that something more than the hours he had studied had enlivened his teaching. When Rachel said that not even her pastor could do any better, Phil replied, "You know, I can't remember the last time I enjoyed anything as much as teaching this lesson. I felt like something took hold of my thoughts and inspired me. I'm not sure it'll happen again."

"Try again next week," kidded Ben, "and we'll let you know. From what I heard tonight, I bet I'll be signing up for the rest of the year, if you'll teach."

That was the start of Phil's teaching ministry. As his own biblical knowledge and experience grew, he came to recognize the role that God played in inspiring his thoughts, providing his energy, and guiding the atmosphere that surrounded his teaching.

Do you have the spiritual gift of teaching?

☐ I like gathering information and then effectively communicating it to others.

☐ I love to study the Bible. I receive new insights and understanding fairly easily and love to share them with people.

☐ When I listen to other teachers, I often think of alternative ways to present the materials.

☐ When I communicate what I have learned, others are motivated to learn more about the Bible and their faith in God.

☐ I want to relate God's truth to life in a way that helps people grow and develop.

☐ When I'm learning a spiritual truth, I automatically envision how to present the concept in a useful way to others.

Suggestions for developing your spiritual gift of teaching:

1. For depth and impact, those with this spiritual gift may need to strengthen their skills in the areas of discernment and wisdom.
2. Even if teaching is one of your spiritual gifts, there is much to be learned by studying teaching methods. This can be accomplished either formally or by observing your favorite teachers.
3. Augment your knowledge and understanding by continuing to seek opportunities to study and share the Bible with others.
4. Create a system for keeping examples, stories, humor, images, quotations, etc., that will enliven your teaching and bring the message home to your listeners.

Biblical Example

Peter and John (Acts 3:11—4:4)

TONGUES AND INTERPRETATION OF TONGUES

A person with the spiritual gift of tongues has the ability to speak in a language, known or unknown to others, supernaturally. A person with the gift of interpretation has the supernatural ability to interpret these spiritual languages.

Biblical Reference: "Now to each one the manifestation of the Spirit is given for the common good . . . to another the ability to speak in different kinds of tongues, and to still another the interpretation of tongues" (1 Corinthians 12:7, 10).

When the day of Pentecost had come, they were all together in one place. And suddenly from heaven there came a sound like the rush of a violent wind, and it filled the entire house where they were sitting. Divided tongues, as of fire, appeared among them, and a tongue rested on each of them. All of them were filled with the Holy Spirit and began to speak in other languages, as the Spirit gave them ability.

Now there were devout Jews from every nation under heaven living in Jerusalem. And at this sound the crowd gathered and was bewildered, because each one heard them speaking in the native language of each. Amazed and astonished, they asked, "Are not all these who are speaking Galileans? And how is it that we hear, each of us, in our own native language? Parthians, Medes, Elamites, and residents of Mesopotamia, Judea and Cappadocia, Pontus and Asia, Phrygia and Pamphylia, Egypt and the parts of Libya belonging to Cyrene, and visitors from Rome, both Jews and proselytes, Cretans and Arabs—in our own languages we hear them speaking about God's deeds of power." All were amazed and perplexed, saying to one another, "What does this mean?" But others sneered and said, "They are filled with new wine." (Acts 2:1–13, NRSV)

Two thousand years later, the general reaction to the gift of tongues has not changed very much. It was as divisive a subject then as it is now. Paul devotes the entire fourteenth chapter of 1 Corinthians to defining the proper role of tongues in the church. This treatment compares to the little explanation present in the rest of Paul's writings of the other spiritual gifts.

Many believe that God uses the gift of tongues to get His message to us by circumventing our rational minds. Experientially, many people have also been given personal prayer languages, sometimes referred to as praying in tongues. In his book *How to Be Pentecostal Without Speaking in Tongues,* Tony Campolo describes the difference:

Speaking in tongues occurs when an individual becomes a "mouthpiece for God" and has a special message from God for the church. The "words" that such a person utters are in an "unknown language." The apostle Paul contends that when someone is exercising this gift, someone should be on hand who has the gift of interpretation (1 Corinthians 12:10). Otherwise, says Paul, all that we have on our hands are some vain babblings. . . .

Praying in tongues is quite another thing. Sometimes the feelings and yearnings of a Christian are so intense and so profound that the ordinary words of human languages cannot express them. There are occasions when what is happening in the mind is so awesome that there are no words in the common vocabulary that can convey its meaning. According to Pentecostals, it is in such times that the individual can become surrendered to God and let the Holy Spirit prompt in him or her prayers and praise in sounds that make no sense to anyone who may be listening. These sounds are not meant to be interpreted because they are not a message from God. Instead these "words" are "groanings" of the heart of the Christian (Romans 8:26).[5]

The gift of tongues is definitely present in the Church today in some form; the important factor is ensuring that it is kept in perspective. Contrary to what some argue, the gift of tongues is not the only sign of "baptism in the Holy Spirit." Paul says, "I thank God that I speak in tongues more than all of you. But in the church I would rather speak five intelligible words to instruct others than ten thousand words in a tongue" (1 Corinthians 14:18–19). Further, many spiritual giants such as John Wesley, George Mueller, and Dwight Moody never spoke in tongues. If you have the gift of tongues, use it for the benefit of the church and your spiritual life. If you do not have it, understand that God does not command us to speak in tongues. The presence of the Holy Spirit is the important thing.

There is also the separate gift of interpretation of tongues. As others hear a person speak in a spiritual tongue, people with the gift of interpretation of tongues can comprehend the language. Many times they understand only the first few words and need to begin interpreting aloud before the rest of the message is revealed to them. As with the spiritual gifts of prophecy, teaching, and wisdom, we are called to test the spirit of what has been said and

---

[5]*How to Be Pentecostal Without Speaking in Tongues*, Tony Compolo, p. 32. © 1991 Word, Inc., Dallas, Texas. All rights reserved.

interpreted before acknowledging it to be true. What God speaks afresh now will never contradict what He has spoken for all times in the Bible.

Do you have the spiritual gift of tongues?

☐ Occasionally I have prayed in language(s) I have never before heard.

☐ Sometimes in prayer, my love for God or my burden for others is so strong that I have difficulty expressing myself in words.

☐ I have been inspired or have inspired others to step out in faith through the use of personal prayer languages.

☐ I find during worship that my tongue wants to express itself in syllables I do not understand.

Suggestions for developing your spiritual gift of tongues:

1. Be aware of our modern bias toward the concrete, material world and its denial of things we cannot see or explain. Allow yourself to be open to this manifestation of the Holy Spirit.

2. Find a prayer group or fellowship where you may operate in this gift and are free to express yourself in this way.

3. Talk to leaders in your Christian fellowship about how they might be open to this expression of faith. Pray for interpreters to be identified.

4. Begin to pray aloud, allowing the tongue to express your feelings.

Do you have the spiritual gift of interpretation of tongues?

☐ I can interpret the words of others who have spoken in languages ("tongues"), even though I have never before heard the languages.

☐ I understand how messages given through the use of tongues serve to glorify God or the church.

☐ When somebody speaks in tongues, I feel the Holy Spirit giving me the ability to interpret or speak.

Suggestions for developing your spiritual gift of interpretation of tongues:

1. Place yourself in atmospheres where the gift of tongues is used (a prayer group, worship services, conference settings).
2. If you believe you have been given the first part of a message, step out in faith and begin to speak that interpretation aloud. Trust God to give you the rest of the meaning as you speak.
3. Ask those around you to give you feedback about the accuracy of your interpretations from their perspectives.

WISDOM

A person with the gift of wisdom has the ability to understand and apply biblical and spiritual knowledge to complex, paradoxical, or other difficult situations.

Biblical Reference: "Now to each one the manifestation of the Spirit is given for the common good. To one there is given through the Spirit the message of wisdom . . ." (1 Corinthians 12:7–8).

For the umpteenth time in two years, church leadership was forced to ponder the topic of location: should the church stay at its inner-city site, despite the increasing problems with vandalism and the deteriorating neighborhood, or should it relocate? Each time, new issues were raised. Each time, more committees were formed to gather more information. Everyone by now knew the alternatives:

- Stay put and pour several hundred thousand dollars into repairs and renovation of the century-old building; or
- Purchase a storefront location that afforded better access for potential members; or
- Rebuild farther south, out of the inner city, and continue an urban ministry by busing people to the new location.

As usual, the discussion was filled with concerns, unanswered questions, and fears about each of the alternatives. When a straw vote was taken, it was clear that the church leadership was not only divided, but overwhelmed and confused by the choices at hand. The meeting's atmosphere grew even more grim as the finance committee reported on best-case and worst-case scenarios.

Finally, Corinne, a long-standing member, got the floor. "It just occurred to me that we have gathered information and discussed the alternatives for *two years*, and most of us are no closer to a decision than we were at the start of the process. I think we have a different, much more crucial problem to solve—that of our faith. Do we have faith that God will continue to guide the future of the church, as He has done so abundantly in the past?

"There are going to be problems and stresses whatever choice we make. The real issue is whether we're ready to take a step in faith and lead this congregation toward its future."

After a silence, one of the committee members said thoughtfully, "That *is* the issue. I've been so afraid of making the 'wrong' choice that I haven't been open to any of the options." Others nodded in agreement. The discussion gradually turned to a celebration of the ways in which God had guided their thriving congregation in the past.

Corinne's words clarified for church leadership that their true obstacle was being willing to move ahead. With that problem out in the open, the location deadlock was finally over. By the end of the next meeting the church leadership was able to flesh out their strategy for moving their church toward its future.

Do you have the spiritual gift of wisdom?

- ☐ It is easy for me to make practical applications of the truths found in the Bible, thinking through different courses of action and determining the best one.
- ☐ People often come to me for advice about personal and religious matters.
- ☐ I am known for my depth of understanding and insights into complex matters.
- ☐ I am often able to find a profoundly simple solution in the midst of a difficult situation.
- ☐ I have resolved paradoxes by cutting through to the essence

of an issue, helping those involved see God's way in the midst of conflicting viewpoints.

Suggestions for developing your spiritual gift of wisdom:

1. James says that "the wisdom that comes from heaven is first of all pure; then peace loving, considerate, submissive, full of mercy and good fruit, impartial and sincere" (James 3:17). You can deepen your understanding of this type of wisdom through extensive study of how to apply the teachings of the Bible to life.
2. Work to continually expose yourself to people and ideas so that you are aware of cultural trends, attitudes, and conflicts.
3. Practice stepping out and trusting some of the gut-level intuitions you have. Then test your solutions with others.
4. Wisdom often improves with spiritual maturity. Nurturing your own spiritual growth can add to the gift of wisdom.

Biblical Example

Peter, Paul, and James at the Council of Jerusalem (Acts 15:5–19)

Drawing Conclusions About Your Spiritual Gifts

Based on reading the Spiritual Gift Descriptions and reading the common characteristics of people with each gift, rate your endowment of each of these spiritual gifts as follows:

5. This is definitely one of my spiritual gifts.
4. This is probably one of my spiritual gifts.
3. I am unsure—I need to learn more about this gift or experiment with ways to use this gift to find out if I have it.
2. This is probably not one of my gifts.
1. This is definitely not one of my gifts.

___ Administration

___ Apostleship

___ Discernment

___ Encouragement/
Counseling

___ Evangelism

___ Faith

___ Giving

___ Healing

___ Helps

___ Hospitality

___ Knowledge

___ Leadership

___ Mercy

___ Miracles

___ Prophecy

___ Shepherding

___ Teaching

___ Tongues

___ Wisdom

Regardless of the ratings you gave each gift, highlight those top three to five gifts that best describe you and record them in LifeKeys Notations, on page 239.

LifeKey 4

If you know yourself, you can find your God-given place.

CHAPTER 4

PERSONALITY TYPES—MELODIES FOR LIFE

Implicit in the command to love one's neighbour as one's self is the duty to love one's self, safeguarded by an equal love of neighbour. Each soul is valued and loved by God, and its individuality or divine image respected. . . . The secret of mature balance will be to accept ourselves as we are and not try to imitate others, and then to rely on God's grace to build us up to the best of which we are capable.[1]

—George Appleton

Picture yourself as a violinist. Do the thoughts of symphonies, concert halls, formal dress, and chamber music appeal to you? Now picture yourself as a fiddler. Are you excited by the thoughts of barn dances, jeans, and toe-tapping fun? Most people express a clear preference for either the violin or the fiddle, yet *they are the same instrument.* We simply call it by a different name when it is used in a different environment. Typically, fiddles aren't played at concert halls, nor are violins played in country western halls. And those who choose to play the violin or the fiddle are attracted to markedly different atmospheres!

Fiddlers and violinists not only play different kinds of music, they interact differently with their audiences, follow different dress codes, and practice in different ways. A few musicians play both "violin" and "fiddle," but most choose one or the other.

God gives us certain preferences, causing certain places or settings to appeal to us, including the places where we worship, work,

---

[1]George Appleton, *Journey for a Soul* (London: William Collins Sons & Co. Ltd., 1976), p. 105.

play, and serve. Much of what appeals to us is dependent on our "personality type." While there are dozens of books on personality type and its various applications—from corporate team building to marriage counseling—here, in these comparatively few pages, we use the concepts of type as a tool for finding the places or atmospheres that most appeal to you.

Your personality type is really your essential nature, the most basic way to describe you and all your assets and strengths. Each type is equally valid and valuable—just like violins and fiddles—but each approaches life in ways different from other types. Imagine it this way: you've always been a fiddler, but some significant person in your life has convinced you to try the violin. So there you are, donning a tuxedo for the first time in your life. You have to follow the director exactly. No picking up the tempo just to see how the dancers handle it. No last-minute changes in the program for audience requests. And no talking or singing allowed while you play! You might think that sounds great—you like order, harmony, and working with others. But you also might wonder if playing your violin in a concert hall is real music. Its precision preempts your style. You could just put on a recording and go home!

Neither kind of music is better or worse, just different. In the same way, no personality type is better or worse, just different in its approach to living. However, if you grew up with siblings or are the parent of more than one child, you know that there can be widespread differences in behavior even within a single family!

Consider two young children from the same family being introduced at a large gathering. The first smiles at no one in particular, then finds a quiet corner to play with the little toy figures she brought in her pocket. The second proceeds to find out the name of every adult in the room, tells two or three of them about his latest escapade, and at last sits on the lap of someone he has persuaded to read him a story. The children have different preferences for how they approach the same situation. They have clearly different personality types.

These differences are natural, God-given aspects of personality. Being who you are—the person God intended you to be—is of paramount importance. No one else has been crafted quite like you! Besides that, the differences make life interesting. Can you imagine what the world would be like if everyone were just like you—your gifts and your shortcomings magnified by the billions?

The Concept of Preferences

To help you understand your unique, God-given personality, we will be using a theoretical construct based on Jungian psychology and popularized through the Myers-Briggs Type Indicator (MBTI®). Carl Jung, the son of a minister, was intensely interested in spiritual matters. A sign over the doorway of his home proclaimed, "Seek Him or not, God is there." Jung saw personality type as a tool through which we can better understand ourselves and therefore deepen that spiritual part of us. Many religious denominations use Jungian theory to help people explore who they are.

Jung theorized that a person's behavior is far from random. When he carefully observed others, patterns emerged that pointed to inherent preferences. To better grasp this concept of preferences, think about your *preferred* hand for writing. Try writing your name and address in the space below with your preferred hand, right or left:

Writing with your preferred hand is easy, natural, and comfortable. Now do the same with your nonpreferred hand:

Note how long it took and how the quality of the output differed. Writing with your nonpreferred hand is awkward, unnatural, or slow. With enough practice, you could improve the output of your less preferred hand. Yet you still gravitate toward the *preferred hand.*

Similarly, we have preferences for how we approach life—how we are energized, how we take in information, how we make decisions, and how we orient our lives. We can *use* any of the preferences, but we *prefer* the ones that are most natural. As we describe each of the eight key preferences, you can keep track of those that seem to describe you best. The preferences are commonly referred to by the following letters:

Energy Source	(E) Extraversion or
	(I) Introversion

Information-processing style	(S) Sensing or
	(N) Intuition[2]
Decision-making style	(T) Thinking or
	(F) Feeling
External lifestye	(J) Judging or
	(P) Perceiving

These eight preferences mix and match for sixteen distinct personality types that can be identified by their four-letter code. Every one of the sixteen personality types has its own strengths and contributions to make to society, the work we do, and the places where we choose to do that work.

If you are energized by other people (you have a preference for Extraversion) you will want to seek places that allow for human interaction. If you like applying what you already know (often true of those with a preference for Sensing) you may want to find a setting where your experience or seniority is valued. These are just two examples of how your personality type can give you insight into choosing both career and service environments.

If you choose tasks, work settings, or occupations that are not a good fit for your personality, you may end up feeling tired and discouraged—like a fiddler trapped in a tux! You may feel fatigue because it is more wearing on you to use your less-preferred processes, much like what you experienced when writing with your nonpreferred hand. You feel discouraged by the fact that even your greater efforts can't match the quality you produce when you use *preferred* processes. Not only that, but if you use your less-preferred processes, you will no doubt find yourself surrounded by people who love what they do, making you feel even more inept or out of place.

So let's learn about the preferences, find the type that best describes you, and apply that information as you think about the settings God causes to appeal to you the most!

How We Are Energized—Extraversion or Introversion

Sandra: *During my graduate studies, I was offered a plum of an internship—great company with a good chance of permanent work,*

---

[2]N is for Intuition because the I is designated for Introversion.

excellent pay, an imposing office with a nice view, and responsibilities in line with my life gifts and my passion for serving others. However, I soon found out that I was only to help people via computer, not face-to-face! In fact, there were only three other people nearby, each in an office fortress similar to my own. When I answered the phone, my voice echoed down the corridor, "Hello, hello, hello, hello…" With no interaction with people, I felt as if I were swimming in pea soup! Give me an interactive, stimulating workspace any day—otherwise, I lose my energy.

When I complained to my co-worker in the next office, she said with surprise, "You're kidding! This is the best situation I've ever had. Lots of peace and quiet, Jenny answering the phones and guarding us against the interruptions that cause me to lose my train of thought ∴ . . . I love it here. This spot was meant just for me!"

People are energized in one of two ways, through *Extraversion* or *Introversion*. Those with a preference for Extraversion enjoy action, interaction, and activity. While not all Extraverts want to be the life of the party, they are still energized by the world around them.

Extraverts tend to function best in environments where they can work as a part of a group or team and where the results are tangible. They are often generalists who possess a breadth of knowledge about many subjects. They process their thoughts by sharing them with others, receiving input, then modifying their ideas based on those interactions.

In contrast, people with a preference for Introversion are energized by their inner world of thoughts and ideas. While as many Introverts jog or bike as Extraverts, they are more likely to be in their inner world, drawing their energy from contemplation, and not from the activity itself.

Introverts tend to prefer settings where they can work alone or one-on-one. Often the fruit of their labor is more conceptual, with a narrower, specialized focus. Their knowledge may run deep in a few selected areas or topics. They prefer to process their thoughts silently, sharing them only when they are well thought through or preferably finalized.

As an Extravert, Sandra struggled with her solitary setting; her co-worker found it ideally suited to her. Some of you may clearly identify with Sandra; others with her co-worker. *Keep in mind that*

Extraversion and Introversion are larger than mere sociability—they relate, in this context, to the concept of energy, not shyness or other social qualities.

As you look through the following lists, think about which word or phrase in each row best describes you (you may wish to check the ones you choose and add up the marks for each preference):

Extraversion	Introversion
☐ Doing; lots going on	☐ Reflecting; one thing going on
☐ Find interruptions stimulating	☐ Find interruptions distracting
☐ Outgoing	☐ Protective
☐ Invite others in	☐ Wait to be invited
☐ Say what they're thinking	☐ Keep thoughts to themselves
☐ Outer energy	☐ Inner energy
☐ Act	☐ Reflect
☐ Live it first	☐ Understand it first
☐ Focus outside	☐ Focus inside
☐ Take over	☐ Step aside

If you are unsure which preference best describes you, place yourself in the story about Sandra. Does her early position fit your idea of a great place to work? Do you share Sandra's opinion of the office space (E), or are you more like her co-worker (I)?

Circle which describes you best:

E (Extraversion)   I (Introversion)

What Gets Your Attention?—Sensing or Intuition

Jane: *Fresh out of college, I worked as a bank examiner. A good bank examiner follows procedures, is detail-oriented, and seldom makes errors of fact. The best examiners do the same thing at each bank in the same way. Good job, high visibility, great place to start a career. However . . . I kept asking, "Why are we doing it this way? What if we tried another procedure? Couldn't we computerize this part so I can avoid making mistakes?" I often annoyed my co-workers with my "hunches" that a bank was doing something wrong and then struggled to provide the step-by-step proof the other examiners needed to understand my hunches. I felt like a troublemaker, even though I was just trying to make things better by finding ways to improve the process. Fortunately, I soon moved to a special projects group where we were* supposed *to look at things differently.*

Another examiner, Don, couldn't understand my choice. "Why would anyone leave? Once you know the ropes, you know exactly *what's expected and the more you do it, the more efficient you become. I enjoy the certainty the job gives me. It's a good job for me." And it was for Don, but not for me.*

There are two ways of perceiving. People with a preference for *Sensing* pay attention to the information gathered through their five senses. Facts, sounds, sights, textures, and details constitute their domain. They are generally good at identifying *what is*, and like settings where they work with actual data that clearly represents factual reality. Career success is perceived to be a progression from entry level through to mastery (as in bank examiner trainee, assistant examiner, examiner, senior examiner, and so on).

In contrast, those with a preference for *Intuition* pay attention to *what could be*—their hunches, analogies, or connections with other knowledge. It's almost as though they rely on their sixth sense more than the other five. Intuitives like places and settings where the emphasis is on new developments and finding possibilities. They define career success as the ability to make career changes as needed (that is, from bank examiner to research specialist to bank controller to consultant).

As an Intuitive, Jane struggled to be a thorough bank examiner and carry on with the tried and true. But for Don, a Sensor, working with the tried and true while trying to improve what *already* works was the road to satisfaction.

As you look through the following lists, which describes you best? Check your choices:

Sensing	**Intuition**
☐ Practical, common sense	☐ Innovative, insightful
☐ Accuracy	☐ Creativity
☐ Use past experience for current work	☐ Use inspiration for current work

☐ Methodical approach
☐ Current reality
☐ Stick with it until you're done
☐ Real world
☐ Applied
☐ Identify pieces
☐ Seen

☐ Novel approach
☐ Future possibilities
☐ Stick with it until you find a better way
☐ Ideal world
☐ Theoretical
☐ Identify connections
☐ Unseen

If you are unsure which preference best describes you, think back to the story of Jane and Don. Do you find you notice and pay attention to things as they are (S), or are you more likely to pay attention to seeing beyond what is (N)? Sensors may say, "A rose is a rose is a rose." Intuitives are more likely to say, "A rose—that makes me think of my high school prom night." Do you enjoy a daily routine (S), or do you constantly look for new possibilities (N)?

Circle which describes you best:

S (Sensing)   N (Intuition)

When Faced With a Decision—Thinking or Feeling

David: *With a father who is a geologist, botanist, and ornithologist rolled into one, my family valued scientific thinking and logical analysis of issues. No hike in the mountains was complete until every plant had been identified down to the genus and species. What could be more natural than for me to head for graduate school in horticulture and agronomy? I had lofty dreams of using my knowledge to fight world hunger.*

I soon found myself the comic relief in an immunology lab amidst a group of logical, task-oriented colleagues. My behavior was probably an instinctive attempt to recover from the scientific procedures I had to follow all day long as I worked with hazardous bacteria cultures. When a new professor announced that the next round of lab work would be the most rigorous yet, I found myself wondering not how I would pass, but how others in the class were feeling about the assignments. Did they fear for their grade-point averages? Would the workload prevent them from coming to the evening Bible study that I taught?

The last straw for my scientific career came that semester in a field where I was supposed to be classifying weeds. Bent over in the hot sun for hours, scribbling numbers in my notebook, alone and very lonely, I almost shouted, "Eureka!" I had the instant recognition that helping people through the Bible studies I taught suited me much more than helping people through the objective, detached gridwork of science.

As I cleaned out my locker, my lab partner remarked, "How can you give this up? We've made such progress on these plant diseases." His mind was set on the logical task at hand, but my heart was in a different place!

Although we are often taught otherwise, there are truly two valid, rational ways of making decisions. People with a preference for *Thinking* like to work in settings that rely on logic, consistency, and fairness when decisions are made. Once they have objectively analyzed the situation, they are ready to proceed. Generally, while thinkers are interested in building relationships with co-workers, they are *more* interested in the tasks at hand. The career of a Thinker often includes goals or milestones such as academic degrees, product innovations, and job titles.

In contrast, people with a preference for *Feeling* include values or priorities in their decision-making process. Often, their values have to do with the needs of the people involved. The Feeler's process is still rational, although not logical. Feelers often consider their business relationships as important as the work they do. They are most at home in settings where they can focus on the needs of people and work in concert with their own personal values. The careers of Feelers need to provide meaning or purpose to themselves or others—they may even turn down promotions if their new responsibilities would remove them too far from their values or the people about whom they care.

While David's life was enriched by his scientific studies (and you should hear him preach using Gerber geranium analogies!), as a Feeler he struggled with the emphasis on finding rational truth instead of meeting people's needs.

In the context of personality, Feeling does not mean *emotional*. It is a larger concept related to decision making. *Feelers can be just as much intellectuals as Thinkers; Thinkers can hold caring values as much as Feelers.* The differences are their priorities and their decision-making style. As you read through the following lists, check the words that describe how you make decisions:

Thinking	Feeling
☐ Logical, analytical	☐ Harmonious, personal
☐ Ideas for data and things	☐ Ideas for people
☐ Fair but firm—few exceptions	☐ Empathetic, making exceptions
☐ Business first	☐ Camaraderie first
☐ Recognition for exceeding requirements	☐ Praise for personal effort
☐ Analyze	☐ Sympathize
☐ Impartial	☐ Subjective
☐ Decide with head	☐ Decide with heart
☐ Find the flaw	☐ Find the positive
☐ Reasons	☐ Values

Now place yourself in David's story. Are you more likely to want to search for truth (T) as scientists and attorneys do, or are you more likely to want to find the most tactful and agreeable outcome to those involved (F), such as counselors and people-oriented professionals do? Are you more excited by the research process (T) or by the people with whom you work (F)? With whom do you most identify?

Circle which best describes you:

T (Thinking)   F (Feeling)

Do You Plan Your Moves or Go With the Flow?—Judging or Perceiving

We like being a team—working together on *LifeKeys*. However, we have slightly different approaches. . . .

Jane, who came to the meeting with a separate file of materials for each chapter, says, "Hey, if we're going to finish this book of eight chapters in four months, let's nail down the structure by this Tuesday. Then we can meet twice a week and finish a chapter every two weeks, okay?"

Sandra and David, who came to the meeting with a blank tablet but heads full of ideas, say, "If we're going to write a book, let's start with a chapter and stay with it until we hit a block or get bored, then move on to another chapter. In fact, let's work on several chapters at the same time up to the *very* deadline and then put it all together. Sounds like enough of a plan to us."

"Yikes," says Jane, "and the worst of it is I know that your ideas really *will* get better the closer we get to the deadline. If only all of those changes didn't have to be made on *my* computer. . . ."

Yes, there are two approaches to life. Those with a preference for *Judging* like to plan their work and work their plan. (Any guesses as to which one of us has a preference for Judging?) Providing organization and structure to any endeavor is truly a calling for Judgers. While not all Judgers organize for the fun of it, they are attracted to places where there is a *reason* for order. Examples might be tax offices (where filing systems are crucial since penalties are substantial) and operating rooms (where disarray can be fatal). They tend to believe that work should come first—only then can they be free to play. A great career, say Judgers, is a planned career.

By comparison, those with a preference for *Perceiving* find that planning can get in the way of living life to the fullest. Perceivers tend to be open and spontaneous as they adapt to what comes their way, and they find environments that call for flexibility ideal. Examples are journalism (where the best reporters are open to late-breaking developments) and building renovation or repair (where no one is certain what the job will entail). Most Perceivers like play to be a part of their work—they try to make life *and* work more fun. Careers that are best, say Perceivers, are those that allow for discovery.

Remember that *Judging in this context does not mean being judgmental, but wanting to come to closure on things. Similarly, Perceiving does not imply that Perceivers are more "perceptive," but that they enjoy the search for more options.*

As you read through the following lists and think about how you like to live your life, check the words that describe you best:

Judging	Perceiving
☐ Organized, efficient	☐ Flexible, multiple tasks
☐ Planned events	☐ Serendipitous events

☐ Stress reduced by planning ahead

☐ Settled and decided

☐ Work before play
☐ Regular, steady effort leads to accomplishment
☐ Systematic
☐ Scheduled
☐ Definite selection
☐ Enjoy finishing

☐ Stress reduced by contingencies

☐ Open to late-breaking information

☐ Work and play coexist
☐ Much is accomplished at the last minute
☐ Spontaneous
☐ Spur of the moment
☐ Several possible choices
☐ Enjoy starting[3]

Now place yourself in our working group. Which approach is most similar to how you approach a task?

Circle which describes you best:

J (Judging)   P (Perceiving)

Based on the above descriptors, what are the preferences (and their letters) that describe you best? These four letters, when combined, form your psychological type. Not to keep any secrets, Sandra and David find that preferences for ENFP describe them best; and Jane, INFJ. Use the spaces below to record your four-letter type:

____ ____ ____ ____

If you are still undecided about which letters to choose, the next sixteen pages give you a description of each type. Read those pages that may describe you. For example, if you think your preferences are for IST but are undecided between the J and the P, read both the ISTJ and ISTP pages.[4]

On those pages you will find several different pieces of information about your type:

• Contribution to Spiritual Community (your special way of

---

[3]Some of the descriptors in these lists reflect the contributions of Ken Green of Green Light Consulting, St. Paul, Minn., and are used with his permission.

[4]To further clarify your preferences, you can take the MBTI,® which is a questionnaire designed to help you sort your preferences on the same four dimensions. Ask your pastor or local community education program for referral to a qualified MBTI® practitioner, or call the publisher of the MBTI,® Consulting Psychologists Press, at 800–624–1765.

adding value to your spiritual community)
- Leadership Style (your way of taking charge)
- Common Confessions (your way of getting off track)
- Order of Preferences (your particular pathway of development)
- Preferred Environment for Service (your places or settings for enhanced effectiveness)
- Possible Spiritual Helps (avenues for deepening your faith)
- Trap (your word of warning)

As you read your type page(s), highlight statements or descriptions that seem to fit you, and put a question mark after things that do not seem to describe you. Remember that *within* each of the sixteen types there is great diversity. At the end of the chapter, we will look at what the Bible hints at concerning personality type, and delve further into settings preferred by various types.

Use the following questions to guide you as you read these pages:

- What factors are important to me as I choose places or settings to work or serve?
- Are there any ways in which my current setting conflicts with my preferences?
- What factors do I want to seek in my next setting to be as effective and satisfied as possible?
- Are there things I can do to change my current setting or my outlook toward it? (You might wish to explore this through your type's "Common Confessions.")

As you discover ways in which your personality type might influence the places or atmospheres you might prefer, record your observations on page 239, LifeKeys Notations.

Prayer

Dear God,

It is great to know that each personality type has value and that through Your Grace You can use us as we are. Help me learn as much as I can about how I operate best and the settings in which I am most comfortable. Show me how my personality can shine for Your purposes. Amen.

ISTJ

Hold them in the highest regard in love because of their work.
1 Thessalonians 5:13

Contribution to the Spiritual Community
- Being dutiful and responsible conservers of tradition
- Having hard-working, dependable, and pragmatic habits
- Using past experience effectively
- Consistently bringing order and logic to all they do

Order of Preferences
1. Sensing
2. Thinking
3. Feeling
4. Intuition

Leadership Style
- Traditional and analytical approach
- Focusing on a daily basis on what needs to be done to keep things "shipshape"
- Adding an efficient and factual perspective to leadership
- Selected by others to lead because of straightforward approach

Preferred Environment for Service
- Individual, hands-on assignments or projects
- Administrative areas, especially organizational, financial, record keeping
- Managing general office tasks to keep things running smoothly
- Overseeing work or doing it themselves

Common "Confessions"
- Not wanting to change the status quo
- Becoming rules-minded and overlooking exceptional needs
- Seeking to know all the nitty-gritty and in the process missing the "big picture"
- Doubting they are "fearfully and wonderfully made," being too aware of areas for self-improvement

Possible Spiritual Helps
- Traditional Bible study
- Daily devotions, contemplation, and prayer
- Reading or hearing about tangible and concrete examples of God's grace in action
- Religious objects which serve as reminders of one's faith

Trap: Being so aware of "works" that they forget they are already saved through grace, not through action

ISTP

But whoever lives by the truth comes into the light so that it may be seen plainly that what he has done has been done through God.
John 3:21

Contribution to the Spiritual Community

- Finding the best way—without red tape—to handle a project
- Contributing quietly, behind the scenes
- Setting up and maintaining automation, computerization
- Being a storehouse of facts and details about their *special* interests

Order of Preferences

1. Thinking
2. Sensing
3. Intuition
4. Feeling

Leadership Style

- Crisp, practical, efficient, as-needed leadership
- Hands-off style unless situation or people call for more
- Perseverance, technical orientation, matched with flexibility and calmness
- Nonhierarchical and egalitarian model for authority

Preferred Environment for Service

- Tasks requiring artisans or craftspeople
- Straightforward, pragmatic, and necessary projects (sidewalk repairs, building upkeep, etc.)
- Involvement with physically oriented or sports ministries
- Crisis intervention—flood and other kinds of disaster relief

Common "Confessions"

- Allowing spiritual life to be more incidental or accidental
- Finding worship or emotional expression of others awkward or even intimidating
- Not factoring the needs of others into daily living
- Trying to reduce everything to a logical formula

Possible Spiritual Helps

- Disciplined quiet study and prayer
- One-on-one spiritual direction with a trusted, like-minded other
- Reading and reflecting about biblical facts and details essential to one's faith
- Being in nature

Trap: Isolating self from spiritual community

ESTP

Therefore everyone who hears these words of mine and puts them into practice is like a wise man who built his house on the rock.
Matthew 7:24

Contribution to the Spiritual Community

- Paying attention to what needs doing/fixing right now
- Meeting practical needs in the most efficient way
- Reminding others of the joys of this life, this *present* time
- Adding a "spark of life" to what they care about; catch the moment and ride the wave!

Order of Preferences

1. Sensing
2. Thinking
3. Feeling
4. Intuition

Leadership Style

- Negotiator, conciliator, or motivator to action
- Bringing order out of chaos, managing distractions well
- Finding the fastest and most direct way to move a task along
- Using an uncanny and exquisite sense of timing when taking charge

Preferred Environment for Service

- Natural crises and disaster relief
- Working with all ages in activity-oriented ministries
- Hands-on projects
- Taking care of physical property

Common "Confessions"

- Questioning reality of religion—hard to take things on faith
- Being skeptical about immortality
- Overlooking spiritual life because of focus on *real* life
- Finding it hard to be patient in dry periods of faith

Possible Spiritual Helps

- In-depth Bible study, focusing on the logical and practical applications of faith
- Quiet time for meditation and rest
- Being in nature
- Spirit-led or charismatic expressions of faith

Trap: Spending too much time in activities, too little in reflection

ESTJ

Be diligent in these matters; give yourself wholly to them.
1 Timothy 4:15

Contribution to the Spiritual Community
- Organizing to meet day-to-day concerns
- Using direct experience/memory of what is most efficient
- Modeling consistent spiritual habits
- Insisting that "hard questions" be answered

Order of Preferences
1. Thinking
2. Sensing
3. Intuition
4. Feeling

Leadership Style
- Traditional, hierarchical style
- Modeling preparedness and efficiency
- Defining and focusing efforts to meet goals
- Marshaling people and tasks in a no-nonsense manner

Preferred Environment for Service
- Management and administration
- Direct, tangible, need-related projects
- Ferreting out problematic areas
- Managing funds according to goals and schedules

Common "Confessions"
- Staying stuck with the tried and true
- Becoming overly rules-bound/ legalistic
- Skeptical—needing proof first
- Missing the wider ramifications of their quick decisions

Possible Spiritual Helps
- Introspection and meditation
- Developing empathy through serving others face-to-face
- Allowing Bible study to influence personal values
- Spending more time with those about whom they care

Trap: Doubting the relevance of even having a faith

ISFJ

**Pursue righteousness, godliness, faith, love, endurance, gentleness.
1 Timothy 6:1, NRSV**

Contribution to the Spiritual Community

- Providing stability, improving efficiency
- Offering a sensible and matter-of-fact attention to daily concerns of people
- Accurately recalling specifics found in conversations and situations
- Adding a sense of dignity and respect to all aspects of the community

Order of Preferences

1. Sensing
2. Feeling
3. Thinking
4. Intuition

Leadership Style

- Encouraging the best from others
- Conscientiously organizing behind the scenes to accomplish tasks
- Enrolling others in a practical, kind, and cooperative way
- Willing to lead *if asked*

Preferred Environment for Service

- Office administration, financial and other record keeping
- Projects focused on health or medical care for others
- Standing committees whose purpose is to provide practical help
- Assisting willingly in any volunteer activity as asked

Common "Confessions"

- Not seeing how all the details add up to become the overall plan
- Retreating from calling attention to selves or claiming their just due
- Avoiding complex and philosophical topics
- Filling time with "all that needs to be done," sometimes neglecting their own spiritual needs

Possible Spiritual Helps

- Spiritual direction for insights as to how God is at work in their lives
- Being in nature to contemplate and sense God's creation
- Structured traditional daily devotions and prayer
- Bible verses that appeal to the senses—the lilies of the field, a single mustard seed, etc.

Trap: Deferring too much to the wants of others

ISFP

Truly I tell you, just as you did it to one of the least of these who are members of my family, you did it to me.
Matthew 25:40, NRSV

Contribution to the Spiritual Community
- Providing loving, gentle, behind-the-scenes help
- Seeing the hand of God in the beauty of nature
- Offering acts of altruistic charity
- Giving immediate, direct, one-on-one help to people in need

Order of Preferences
1. Feeling
2. Sensing
3. Intuition
4. Thinking

Leadership Style
- Leading directly only when they have crucial knowledge or when no one else will
- Taking responsibility by doing needed detail and follow-through
- Considerate, compassionate, tolerant, and forgiving
- Flexible and open to needs of the present

Preferred Environment for Service
- Nursery, preschool, those with special needs, and elder care
- Prayer and healing
- Practical support to needy others
- Participating in craft and artistic endeavors

Common "Confessions"
- May not take credit that is due, and may be too modest for their own good
- Sacrificing self to greater welfare
- Avoiding firm stand *until* values are crossed—then watch out!
- Not making appropriate demands on others

Possible Spiritual Helps
- Selecting role models for the kind of spiritual life sought
- Being in nature, meditating on God in natural things; experiencing *true* leisure—time alone for reflection
- Trying charismatic worship styles
- Joining a small group to add structure to spiritual journey

Trap: Not valuing self highly enough

ESFP

A cheerful heart is good medicine.
Proverbs 17:22

Contribution to the Spiritual Community
- Reminding others how to appreciate the wonders of God through one's five senses
- Bringing enjoyment to all
- Being generous with time and talents
- Adding warmth, excitement, and fun to endeavors

Order of Preferences
1. Sensing
2. Feeling
3. Thinking
4. Intuition

Leadership Style
- Attracting others by enthusiasm, optimism, and zest
- Energizing people to start a task
- Seeking input from all involved before making a binding decision
- Facilitating conflict and crises through a warm and personal approach

Preferred Environment for Service
- Tangible acts of service for others such as decorating, providing flowers, or arranging transportation
- Youth, young adult, sports, and action-oriented ministries
- Visitation of sick and elderly
- Planning and staffing community-building celebrations or gatherings

Common "Confessions"
- Neglecting to make time for God and Spirit-filled matters
- Not giving enough thought to future concerns
- Being too generous or giving too much of self to others
- Not wanting to act alone

Possible Spiritual Helps
- Group devotions or study time
- Looking for concrete experiences of God in daily life
- Biblical study for applications to one's own life
- Considering both the positive and negative sides of spiritual offerings

Trap: Trying to please everyone at the same time

ESFJ

**For I am not seeking my own good but the good of many,
so that they may be saved.
1 Corinthians 10:33**

Contribution to the Spiritual Community
- Preserving the faith from one generation to the next
- Offering a service orientation, warmth and caring
- Making people feel welcome and valued
- Knowing what matters for people and organizations

Order of Preferences
1. Feeling
2. Sensing
3. Intuition
4. Thinking

Leadership Style
- Traditional take-charge yet take-care style
- Building relationships into coalitions to accomplish tasks
- Including others' opinions and inviting them into direct service
- Following a cooperative, consensual, and timely plan to get things done

Preferred Environment for Service
- Hospitality responsibilities (welcoming, decorations, social activities, etc.)
- Visiting with the elderly, sick, shut-ins
- Organizing food shelves, day-care shelters, recovery groups, etc.
- Administrating youth, education, or social organizations

Common "Confessions"
- Telling others what they ought/should be doing
- Sweeping conflicts under the rug to maintain harmony
- Caretaking until others lose interest in providing for their own needs
- Being reluctant to question tradition or leaders

Possible Spiritual Helps
- Group Bible study with applications to daily life
- Evangelism and other outreach programs
- Retreats with others where emphasis is on Christian fellowship
- Reading/hearing accounts of grace in the lives of others

Trap: Focusing so much on others that they overlook their own feelings and needs

INFJ

**Therefore encourage one another and build each other up,
just as in fact you are doing.**
1 Thessalonians 5:11

Contribution to the Spiritual Community

- Understanding the feelings and motivations of others
- Finding creative ways for people to accomplish tasks, making the process enjoyable
- Modeling integrity and follow-through
- Lending future-oriented ideas to planning and development

Order of Preferences

1. Intuition
2. Feeling
3. Thinking
4. Sensing

Leadership Style

- Developing an atmosphere of mutual trust
- Working for cooperation rather than demanding it
- Inspiring others with their goals and plans for attaining them
- Acting as facilitators

Preferred Environment for Service

- Ministries that seek to help others grow and develop
- Spiritual direction or one-on-one counseling
- Using words, oral or written, to influence outcomes for people
- Small group leadership

Common "Confessions"

- Finding it difficult to ask others for help
- Reluctantly advocating for their ideas or talents
- Focusing with such intensity on their own "vision" that they miss the suggestions of others
- Withholding needed criticism to maintain harmony

Possible Spiritual Helps

- Journaling and poetic writing
- Finding an "encourager," someone who will listen to ideas and suggest taking action
- Using creative imagery to make Scripture come alive
- Time alone to reflect, meditate, and pray

Trap: Trying to work things out alone, being hesitant or afraid to ask for the help of others

INFP

Do not conform any longer to the pattern of this world, but be transformed by the renewing of your mind.
Romans 12:2

Contribution to the Spiritual Community
- Bringing a compassionate, caring, and personal focus to those places they serve
- Adding a spirit of harmony
- Reminding others of their ideals and the worthiness of striving to meet them
- Providing a positive vision for the future

Order of Preferences
1. Feeling
2. Intuition
3. Sensing
4. Thinking

Leadership Style
- Facilitating people and processes
- Persuading through their convictions and inspiring others to do what is right
- Working with individuals to reach their fullest potential
- Holding people and organizations accountable to values; providing integrity

Preferred Environment for Service
- One-on-one counseling/ coaching
- Prayer partners
- Areas where they can add creative ideas
- Ministries that make use of the fine arts

Common "Confessions"
- Taking negative feedback personally, needing too much positive support
- Believing that others do not *care* enough
- Avoiding issues where conflict may emerge *unless* a value is crossed—then a tiger emerges!
- Coming across to others as too idealistic and impractical

Possible Spiritual Helps
- Reading and identifying with the compassionate "giants" of faith
- Prayer partners and prayer circles
- Contemplation and meditation
- Inspirational music, books, and symbols

Trap: Being entrenched in one's ideals

ENFP

Whatever is true, whatever is noble, whatever is right, whatever is pure, whatever is lovely, whatever is admirable—if anything is excellent or praiseworthy—think about such things.
Philippians 4:8

Contribution to the Spiritual Community
- Offering warmth and enthusiasm
- Adding vision and zest to community undertakings
- Sharing resources, especially people and books
- Valuing widespread interests and relationships

Order of Preferences
1. Intuition
2. Feeling
3. Thinking
4. Sensing

Leadership Style
- Using personal charm and charisma to get others started
- Motivating and encouraging people to do their best
- Advocating for the less fortunate
- Providing ingenious ideas

Preferred Environment for Service
- Missions or service-related projects that involve building relationships
- Evangelism, public speaking, promoting
- Liaison to other service organizations/groups, especially those with a creative focus
- Youth work, multicultural and diverse environments

Common "Confessions"
- Overcommitting—so many needs, so little time
- Neglecting to give attention to personal, physical, and emotional needs
- Learning just enough about a subject to be "dangerous" or to get by
- Not following through before moving on

Possible Spiritual Helps
- Methodical spiritual disciplines (prayer, study, worship, etc.)
- Singing, acting, dancing, being out in the natural world
- Spiritual study, discussion, or fellowship with small groups
- Self-reflection to get in touch with own feelings

Trap: Being attracted to the newest, latest, most intriguing . . .

ENFJ

"For I know the plans I have for you," says the Lord, "plans to prosper you and not to harm you, plans to give you hope and a future."
Jeremiah 29:11

Contribution to the Spiritual Community
- Monitoring values and integrity
- Supporting others with warmth and encouragement
- Believing in the positive nature of people
- Inviting others to live up to their ideals

Order of Preferences
1. Feeling
2. Intuition
3. Sensing
4. Thinking

Leadership Style
- Large-scale organizing using the best people have to offer
- Planning for the future needs of the group or community
- Modeling exemplary behavior
- Being willing to personally dig in to accomplish the task at hand

Preferred Environment for Service
- Preaching, adult and children's education, sharing one's faith via oral communication
- Greeting newcomers, creating inclusive atmospheres
- Structuring ministries to target the large-scale needs of people
- Organizing fellowship activities and providing a sense of harmony and fun

Common "Confessions"
- Becoming too personally involved in the success or failure of endeavors
- Assuming their way is the most noble or altruistic
- Keeping conflict under wraps in favor of harmony, not wanting to ruffle feathers
- Taking the weight of the world on their shoulders

Possible Spiritual Helps
- Personal quiet time with God
- Rest and spiritual retreat to remove responsibilities and focus on personal faith
- Studying the lives of biblical and other spiritual leaders for insights into their *personal* lives
- Meeting with others in mutual authenticity, looking past the "shoulds" to encourage and honestly affirm each other

Trap: Avoiding the expression of negative feelings that might result in disharmony—even in relationship with God.

INTJ

**I devoted myself to study and to explore by wisdom
all that is done under heaven.**
Ecclesiastes 1:13

Contribution to the Spiritual Community

- Envisioning systems to create a better world
- Breaking new ground, shifting paradigms, and changing the way people view things
- Designing or adjusting strategies and structures for future needs
- Thinking and acting independently from traditional or outmoded ways

Order of Preferences

1. Intuition
2. Thinking
3. Feeling
4. Sensing

Leadership Style

- Being a force for change by virtue of the power of their ideas
- Challenging self and others to work toward a compelling future
- Developing conceptual designs and models
- Seeing patterns and systems which solve complex problems

Preferred Environment for Service

- Spiritual coaching and direction
- Teaching, especially adults
- Long-range planning and strategy development
- Finding new approaches with wide ramifications for traditional ministries

Common "Confessions"

- Reluctant to share real self with others
- Wanting to find answers to everything that interests or concerns them
- Not feeling as competent as they'd like
- Expecting others to "see" the future as they do

Possible Spiritual Helps

- Spiritual direction to address specific issues
- Intellectual study, dialogue or debate on matters of faith, especially with experts
- Contemplation, reflection, and meditation
- Silent or directed spiritual retreats

Trap: Being lost in thought—not mindful of others or situation

INTP

And this is my prayer: that your love may abound more and more in knowledge and depth of insight.
Philippians 1:9

Contribution to the Spiritual Community

- Relentlessly searching for truth in all things spiritual
- Finding out the long-term consequences of any given plan or strategy for action
- Pointing out errors of logic or sentimentality
- Providing clear, analytical frameworks for understanding

Order of Preferences

1. Thinking
2. Intuition
3. Sensing
4. Feeling

Leadership Style

- Winning respect through depth of knowledge
- Demonstrating ability to conceptualize an issue
- Influencing through theoretical ideas
- Making decisions from a sound, logical foundation

Preferred Environment for Service

- Providing an orderly approach to exploring spiritual issues
- Scholarly or intellectual endeavors
- Conceptualizing or blueprinting an outreach, ministry, or service effort
- Program review and development

Common "Confessions"

- Getting too caught up in skepticism
- Attempting to intellectualize faith to the exclusion of the heart
- Ignoring physical and other tangible needs until problems arise
- Underestimating the personal needs of others, overriding their concerns

Possible Spiritual Helps

- Intellectually demanding and challenging Bible study
- Spiritual resources which demonstrate logically the principles of faith
- Reflection, prayer, and meditation
- Spiritual direction with accountability for continuing their Christian growth

Trap: Not realizing how they are coming across, especially when in pursuit of truth

ENTP

Not that I have already obtained this or have already reached the goal; but I press on to make it my own, because Christ Jesus has made me his own.
Philippians 3:12, NRSV

Contribution to the Spiritual Community

- Initiating new projects, direction, etc., with enthusiasm and energy
- Meeting challenges proactively
- Providing insight and imagination to tasks and projects
- Exhibiting resourcefulness with strategies and structures

Order of Preferences

1. Intuition
2. Thinking
3. Feeling
4. Sensing

Leadership Style

- Using models and logical systems to meet needs
- Speaking out for change
- Organizing, operating, and assuming the risk for new ideas and approaches
- Challenging and encouraging personal and/or organizational achievement

Preferred Environment for Service

- Liaison to other service groups, especially those with a novel or unusual focus
- World service and missions
- Strategy development for congregations and missions
- Marketing and promoting spiritual needs and services

Common "Confessions"

- Overselling the benefits, forgetting or omitting the bare, cold facts
- Taking ownership of tasks from others, overextending one's boundaries
- Believing that what is so easily imagined can be easily achieved
- Not following procedures, ignoring rules

Possible Spiritual Helps

- Methodical spiritual disciplines
- Challenging, intellectually vigorous Bible study
- Corporate worship
- *Personal* relationship with God

Trap: Competitiveness

ENTJ

Dear children, let us not love with words or tongue
but with actions and in truth.
1 John 3:18

Contribution to the Spiritual Community

- Developing long-range plans for people and organizations
- Understanding how parts relate to whole
- Bringing a logical order to problems
- Intellectual and philosophical insights applied to spiritual matters

Order of Preferences

1. Thinking
2. Intuition
3. Sensing
4. Feeling

Leadership Style

- Taking charge when a strong leader is needed
- Using conceptual models to guide action
- Exhibiting dedication, concentration, confidence
- Standing firm on principles against opposition

Preferred Environment for Service

- Leadership, long-range planning, strategic alignment or development of mission
- Fund-raising and investing
- Program evaluation and development
- Adult education

Common "Confessions"

- Railroading gentler types
- Overly rational, wanting to reduce everything to a logical formula or principle
- Holding to rigorous standards for self and others
- Being impatient and critical

Possible Spiritual Helps

- Intellectually oriented Bible study
- Discussion/dialogue with a respected spiritual leader
- Contemplation and prayer to build a more personal relationship with God
- Inquiry and learning through exploration of theological questions

Trap: Not being open to the influence of others

Are Personality Types a Biblical Concept?

People frequently ask the question, "Is it is really biblical that we have a personality type? Can't God change who we are?" While there is no specific Bible passage that states that God has given us each a certain personality type, looking at people in the Bible confirms that much of our personality is as inborn as the color of our eyes or the size of our feet. Now that you have a basic understanding of the preferences, let's look at the apostle Paul as an example of what we mean.

We have just a few glimpses of Paul prior to his conversion to Christianity—the time when he was known as Saul. In the book of Acts we find him

- waging a campaign against the Church, getting letters from the high priest to grant him legal authority to persecute Christians (Acts 9:1–2).
- standing by at the stoning of Stephen, approving of the crowd's actions (Acts 7:58–60).
- dragging Christians off to prison himself (Acts 8:3).

From these texts, we get hints of a man of action, probably with a preference for Extraversion. Not content to merely criticize or plot against the Christians, he was one of the five-star generals leading the frontal attack!

We can also infer that Paul had a preference for Intuition, given his big-picture approach to destroying the Church. His scholarship and standing, often evident in those with a preference for Thinking, gave him access to government officials—and credibility when he spoke. His quickness of action, finally, may point toward a Judging lifestyle, planned and conclusive in its results.

Paul's conversion to Christianity brought about drastic changes in his life. The man who once led the persecution of the early Church was now its foremost advocate, devoting his life to spreading the new faith. As profound as this change was, however, look at his actions and see if they are still consistent with what we *surmise* were ENTJ preferences:

- He argued effectively for the new religion using the logical methods of the Jewish faith (T).
- He had a grand-scale scheme for spreading the gospel by speaking first to the Jews and then to the Gentiles (N).

- He traveled, spoke, and taught to spread the faith widely (E).
- He was decided in his beliefs, actively seeking closure on many of the debated issues facing the young Church (J).

Can you see the same visionary ability in his methods of preaching first to the Jews and then to the Gentiles? The same boldness and knowledge that gave him confidence with the greatest authorities of his day? The same sureness in his positions? The same desire to bring closure to issues and debate? These are the essence of Paul's personality type—the personality that made him so effective in opposing the Church also eventually made him one of its most effective advocates. His probable ENTJ style that drove him to attack the Church now allowed him to pen the words of his new conviction:

> For I am convinced that neither death nor life, neither angels nor demons, neither the present nor the future, nor any powers, neither height nor depth, nor anything else in all creation, will be able to separate us from the love of God that is in Christ Jesus our Lord. (Romans 8:38–39)

As a likely ENTJ, Paul probably would have found it awkward to embrace a quiet role and place in the early Church. His personality type and gifts catapulted him to the forefront of whatever he was doing. He was the type of leader God needed at the time, embracing the whole civilized world in his attempts to spread Christianity.

Paul's probable ENTJ personality type, however, is not the only kind that God uses for leadership. A study of Mother Teresa, for example, might reveal her decision-making style based more on her values and feelings (F), with energy gained more through solitude or one-to-one ministry (I).

For each of us, our personalities play a determining role in where we can be most effective. In an old story, a person asked his rabbi how to become acceptable to God. The rabbi replied, "We become acceptable not by being more like Moses, but by becoming who God meant *us* to be." Personality type is a wonderful tool to help you understand not only yourself but those around you. Understanding enables us to respect those who are different from us, even as we respect ourselves.

A Few Other Facts About Type

- *Am I born to be a certain type?*
  While most believe that type is inborn, outside factors can influence our preferences. For example, we might be born into a family or culture that does not nourish a particular type; if you are the only Feeler in a family of Thinkers, you may be conditioned to find logical support for decisions. If you are the only Thinker in a family of Feelers, you may learn the most considerate ways to express your objective analyses. Some of us therefore may find it hard to select what God truly *meant* for us to be, as opposed to what others thought we *should* be.

- *Can I work to change my preferences?*
  Yes, with some difficulty you could. But your preferences celebrate who you are. No preference or type is better than another, just different. While we all can take cues from each of the preferences and can learn to compensate for some of our weaknesses, it makes more sense to concentrate the bulk of our energy on working out of our strengths. If we are all gifted but merely gifted in different ways, then the best type to be is your own!

- *Are all people in one type alike?*
  While there are some similarities among people of the same type, type doesn't explain *everything* about you or anyone else. For example, while David and Sandra as ENFPs are attracted toward rather global schemes for helping others, Sandra does not share David's interests in science. Further, type does not measure ability or competency in any area. It does, however, do an excellent job of helping you understand yourself, appreciate others, know the work/service setting that is best for you, and make sense of some of your life choices.

- *My type has trouble with time management (or interpersonal niceties or accuracy, etc.) Can I use my type as an excuse?*
  Blaming your type is a poor excuse for any inexcusable behavior! Instead, your type can give you insights into your trouble spots, a reason behind the struggle that you can put to use to compensate for your performance in that area. For example, a Perceiver who constantly struggles to finish projects might learn to set deadlines for each step of a process rather than focusing on a single completion date, and an Introvert may find

that speaking out early is the most appropriate thing to do in some instances.

- *Should I base my career on my type?*
Personality type should not necessarily discourage you from choosing an area of work. Research any given field, work setting, or task—if it still appeals to you, enter it. Know, however, that your perspective on many things may be different from the majority of your co-workers. Entering an occupation with this knowledge is far different from *not* understanding why you might feel like an outsider. Often, the person whose personality preferences are atypical for a given profession can bring new insights to everyone precisely because he or she differs from the group. Jane, for example, did a good job as one of the few Intuitive bank examiners and made a few suggestions that streamlined the tried-and-true examination process.

Using Type to Find the Settings Which God Has Caused to Appeal to You the Most

Within each psychological type, Jung saw a hierarchy for personal development. Each preference has a *dominant* function, the one we find most easy to use. The dominant function, listed as (1) in the chart below, develops early in life. Because of this, your dominant function (S, N, T or F) can be the greatest source of your gifts. Sometimes because people are so *accustomed* to their dominant function, they overlook its power or the fact that others might truly marvel at what to them seems only natural! If your dominant function involves the way you take in information (Sensing or Intuition), then your *auxiliary,* or number (2) function, involves your way of making decisions (Thinking or Feeling), and vice versa.

The auxiliary function also develops early in life and provides necessary balance to the way you live. Sensing or Intuition as an auxiliary keeps a dominant Thinking or Feeling person from deciding without enough information (often the route of close-mindedness). On the other hand, an auxiliary of Thinking or Feeling can help a dominant Sensing or Intuitive person focus and complete what they observe. (An inadequate Thinking or Feeling auxiliary can be the route to aimlessness and procrastination for people who are Sensing or Intuitive.)

The preferences that are numbered (3) and (4) often lag in development or are sometimes not experienced fully until the second half of life, if at all. This hierarchy of preferences for each type offers clues to the settings that people of that type often automatically seek or avoid.

In choosing the best settings for you, find your type on the following table. Take to heart the suggestions for your dominant and auxiliary preferences as you look for settings that appeal to you—and cautiously enter those settings that require the third and fourth preferences!

ISTJ	ISFJ	INFJ	INTJ
1. Sensing	1. Sensing	1. Intuition	1. Intuition
2. Thinking	2. Feeling	2. Feeling	2. Thinking
3. Feeling	3. Thinking	3. Thinking	3. Feeling
4. Intuition	4. Intuition	4. Sensing	4. Sensing
ISTP	ISFP	INFP	INTP
1. Thinking	1. Feeling	1. Feeling	1. Thinking
2. Sensing	2. Sensing	2. Intuition	2. Intuition
3. Intuition	3. Intuition	3. Sensing	3. Sensing
4. Feeling	4. Thinking	4. Thinking	4. Feeling
ESTP	ESFP	ENFP	ENTP
1. Sensing	1. Sensing	1. Intuition	1. Intuition
2. Thinking	2. Feeling	2. Feeling	2. Thinking
3. Feeling	3. Thinking	3. Thinking	3. Feeling
4. Intuition	4. Intuition	4. Sensing	4. Sensing
ESTJ	ESFJ	ENFJ	ENTJ
1. Thinking	1. Feeling	1. Feeling	1. Thinking
2. Sensing	2. Sensing	2. Intuition	2. Intuition
3. Intuition	3. Intuition	3. Sensing	3. Sensing
4. Feeling	4. Thinking	4. Thinking	4. Feeling

Note your top two preferences, and seek settings that honor:

Sensing: Places where factual details and accuracy are important.

Intuition: Places where insight and imagination are important.

Thinking: Places where objectivity and logic are important.

Feeling: Places where personal values and their impact on people are important.

Now look at your third or fourth preferences and enter with caution settings that utilize:

Sensing: Places where factual details and accuracy are important.

Intuition: Places where insight and imagination are important.

Thinking: Places where objectivity and logic are important.

Feeling: Places where personal values and their impact on people are important.[5]

Letting Type Structure Your Search

As you try to find the setting God most desires for you, your type can aid your search process. Here are some guidelines for finding the settings that respect your particular preferences:

If you have a preference for Extraversion, find the right setting for you by visiting different sites, talking to friends who operate in an environment you would like to try, and using your network of family, friends, church members, and colleagues in your profession or work. *Remember,* however, to listen as much as you talk. Guard against overextending yourself, since Extraverts often mistake activity for results. (Too many visits, conversations, and networks can leave you unfocused.)

If you have a preference for Introversion, do library research about settings you find appealing. Journal or reflect on the factors that can contribute to your finding your niche. *Remember,* however, that you'll need to act and perhaps move beyond your comfort zone in reaching out to others who can help you when the time is right. Be careful to consider how you can sell yourself once you've reached some conclusions.

If you have a preference for Sensing, collect specific information about what settings available to you right now match your education, experience, and economic and family needs. To find your niche, use what you have learned from your past about what works and doesn't work for you. *Remember,* however, to be willing to take a risk if you need to and try something new—even if you don't have 100% of what is required (80% will generally do!). Try not

---

[5]For further information, see *Work It Out,* by Hirsh with Kise. Palo Alto, Calif.: Davies-Black Publishing, 1996.

to let security needs force you to settle for less than what you want. Consider the long-term implications both for staying where you are or going to something less known.

If you have a preference for Intuition, brainstorm all the possibilities that match your future aspirations and dreams. Try out—even if only in your mind—some of those far-fetched ideas or unusual opportunities you dream up. Don't worry about staying on one track, as your penchant is for change and novelty. *Remember,* however, not to stretch credulity too far by overlooking important requirements or getting caught up in too many possibilities.

If you have a preference for Thinking, use a matrix listing several settings to be evaluated according to criteria important to you—commute time, economic and family needs, potential career growth, and so on. Or use a system of pros and cons to analyze various settings available to you. *Remember,* however, to consider your own personal needs and values and those of the people who are most important to you and to factor in your subjective response as well.

If you have a preference for Feeling, think of people you admire or would like to emulate. Where possible, seek them out to hear about what they like in their setting and how they found their niche. Factor in your key values to see if they are in harmony in a particular setting. *Remember,* however, that for Feelers there must be a purpose beyond the paycheck. Be sure to please *yourself* as well as your significant others in your selection.

If you have a preference for Judging, create an organized plan complete with a "to-do" list, examining what potential setting would work best for you. Make a timetable that has step-by-step activities to help narrow the options. *Remember,* however, not to hone in and decide too quickly, without thorough exploration of what is available to you. Ask yourself, "Have I asked enough questions, gathered enough data, and stayed open long enough in this process?" Sometimes patience takes practice!

If you have a preference for Perceiving, give yourself a generous length of time to gather information and explore options. Take detours in your process to see if anything interesting turns up. As new information comes along, capture it and see what it tells you about the setting where you'll most clearly thrive. *Remember,* however, that others may have trouble with what might seem to be (or actually is!) procrastination. Ultimately, the situation may *force* you to decide!

Sample Settings by Preferences

(Caution: This is a *limited* list of possible settings in alphabetical order and is meant only to illustrate the preference, not severely narrow your choices.)

Extraversion:
- Banking
- Construction
- Entertainment
- Food service
- Home economics
- Hospitality
- Insurance
- Marketing
- Public relations
- Sales

Introversion:
- Computer science
- Engineering
- Higher education
- Law
- Libraries
- Mechanical fields
- Medicine
- Publishing
- Research and development
- Scientific fields

Sensing:
- Administration
- Agriculture
- Building and trades
- Food service
- Law enforcement
- Maintenance
- Manufacturing
- Navigation
- Nursing
- Public service

Intuition:
- Artistic fields
- College or university teaching
- Consulting
- Entertainment
- Law
- Photography
- Psychology
- Religion
- Research
- Social services

Thinking:
- Agriculture
- Banking
- Building and trades
- Chemistry
- Computer science
- Engineering
- Law
- Management
- Research
- Science

Feeling:
- Administrative areas
- Artistic fields
- Counseling
- Health services
- Hospitality
- In-home service providers
- Libraries
- Physical therapy
- Preschool or elementary schools
- Religious organizations

Judging:
- Building and trades
- Chemistry
- Finance
- Health care management
- Home management
- Sales management
- Restaurant management
- Teaching
- Public service
- Jurisprudence

Perceiving:
- Artistic fields
- Child care
- Counseling
- Crafts or trades
- Entertainment
- Food service
- Journalism
- Psychology
- Research
- Surveying

LifeKey 5

Seek the values that strike the right chord with God.

CHAPTER 5

VALUES—CHORDS THAT TOUCH YOUR SOUL

We choose—either to live our lives or to let others live them for us. By making and keeping promises to ourselves and to others, little by little we increase our strength until our ability to act is more powerful than any of the forces that act upon us.[1]

—Stephen Covey

Think about the music you most enjoy, be it jazz, rock, or symphonic. If the notes of a chord are played correctly, *harmony* results. If the wrong notes are played, you hear disharmony or *discord*—a word that applies not just to dissonance in music, but to conflict or lack of agreement among people or ideas.

Each of us has places or settings that harmonize with what we believe in or value. They play our kind of music. You can feel discord, however, without being sure of the source of the bad notes—not just in music but at work, church, or home. Identifying what you value highly can help you sort the right notes from the ones that make you want to cover your ears!

Pete, for instance, had known for a long time that his work was no longer satisfying for him. When he interviewed for his current position, the manager told him that he would be assigned to new product development. However, within months of being hired, the

---

[1]Reprinted with the permission of Simon & Schuster from *First Things First,* by Stephen R. Covey, A. Roger Merrill, and Rebecca R. Merrill. Copyright © 1994, by Stephen R. Covey, A. Roger Merrill, and Rebecca R. Merrill.

job was reengineered. He instead found himself glued to a computer with an overflow of administrative tasks from his boss—and reviewing legal contracts to find inconsistencies, of all things!

When his prayer group decided to do a values exercise together, Pete was not wild about the idea. Now, though, as they sat together sorting values cards, he found himself absorbed in the choices he was making.

"Accuracy—I have to value that in my job, and in serving others. Competency—I want to do things right . . . and I want my religious beliefs to be well thought through . . ." A moment later Pete drew a quick breath and his friends looked up at him. Pete said eagerly, "This tells me what's wrong with my life right now! Look—most of the values I placed under 'These are very valuable' are there because my job *forces* me to be that way. If I were to sort values outside of my work situation, the order would change drastically. Look, creativity has been knocked right out of my priorities. The same with friendships—I'm simply too busy! Sorting these values cards points to exactly why I'm so miserable in this job."

What Are Values?

What do you value? Think of the things that

- feel important to you,
- define your fundamental character,
- supply meaning to your work and life,
- influence the decisions you make,
- compel you to take a stand,
- provide an atmosphere in which you are most productive.

You may not know what you value until an event, circumstance, or person comes into direct conflict with that value—or, until you purposefully try to identify what is important to you, as Pete and his prayer group did. Values are another *LifeKey* that provide clues to who you are, why you're here, and what you do best.

Values can differ significantly even among people who would seem to hold similar goals. Let's look at one rather famous values statement:

> We hold these truths to be self-evident; that all men are created equal; that they are endowed by their creator with cer-

tain unalienable rights; that among these are life, liberty, and the pursuit of happiness. . . .

When Thomas Jefferson penned these words in the Declaration of Independence, he assumed that those he represented (British colonists living in America without governmental representation) agreed with him that the rights to life, liberty, and the pursuit of happiness were of such high value that people would be willing to die for them. These shared values pulled together the ragtag Continental Army, sustained it through years of fighting and deprivation, and allowed it to outlast the army of the British, one of the finest in the world. Teaming up with people who hold values similar to yours can make it easier to overcome difficulties as well as find purpose and meaning in what you do.

Yet even as you skimmed the words above, you might have questioned whether what Jefferson penned catches the essence of what is most valuable in life *today*. As times and circumstances change, so do people's values. No matter where we live, we will find neighbors and fellow citizens whose values clash with ours.

Within the Christian faith there are certain values with which few would quibble—we are to love God above all else and love our neighbors as ourselves. Yet there are other values that people of faith may disagree about—what a value means and how important it is. And while our core Christian values may be similar, varying life circumstances may affect how we prioritize other values. If you are facing job transition, for example, you may place a much higher value on security than you did even a year ago. Our values may encourage us to choose *different* but *acceptable* paths.

Do We Really Have the Option to Order Our Values?

We have discovered that God has given us life gifts, spiritual gifts, and a personality type. While the Bible has a lot to say about values, God wants to shape how we define, prioritize, and live out our own personal values. This is in contrast to life gifts (which are to be developed), spiritual gifts (which are to be discovered), and personality types (which are to be understood).

From the Declaration of Independence, for instance, we can assume that liberty or freedom is highly valued in America. Indeed it is, even two hundred years after the document was written.

Many of us would define freedom as the ability to do as we please. From a biblical perspective, however, that is not freedom. It can be bondage to sin. Biblically, true freedom releases us to follow Christ, not to run after whatever we please.

While there are definitely values by which all Christians must abide, two individuals can meet similar challenges with different responses, finding their own solutions that are both biblically sound and reflective of who they are and what they value most.

For example, meet Ruth, a Moabite woman of the Old Testament. She and her sister-in-law, Orpah, had the good fortune to marry into a kindly family of foreigners from Judah. This family had settled nearby to escape the famine in their homeland. Although the husbands of Ruth and Orpah died, the two women remained with their mother-in-law, Naomi, a woman from Judah. Naomi had no more sons for Ruth and Orpah to marry, as custom would have dictated. The culture left the two young women free to return to their own families.

Naomi was ready to go home, having received word that the famine was finally over. She told Ruth and Orpah to return to their parents' homes, believing that they would be happiest there, but they begged to remain with her. When she reminded them that their chances of remarriage were slim if they stayed with her, Orpah agreed to go home, but Ruth refused:

> "Look," said Naomi, "your sister-in-law is going back to her people and her gods. Go back with her."
> But Ruth replied, "Don't urge me to leave you or to turn back from you. Where you go I will go, and where you stay I will stay. Your people will be my people and your God my God." (Ruth 1:15–16)

This was a very painful decision for both daughters-in-law. Orpah obviously loved Naomi, placing a high value on the relationship they had built, but her final decision rested on other values: perhaps her family of origin, the geographic location where she had lived almost all her life, or tradition. The Bible expresses no opinion on the way Orpah prioritized her values. She is portrayed as a caring individual who found the decision of whether or not to leave Naomi a difficult choice.

Ruth held a different set of core values. To her, maintaining the relationship with her mother-in-law and the religious beliefs she had accepted outweighed the loss of her homeland and culture.

We know that Ruth's decision ultimately led to security in a new marriage, a marriage that established the family line that led to the birth of King David. We don't know whether Orpah found happiness, but the Bible does *not* express that Orpah made a bad choice. Ruth and Orpah's values were different, bringing them to choose different futures.

Why Clarify Your Values?

In the movie *Chariots of Fire*, Olympic runner Eric Liddell tells his sister, "Jenny, when I run, I feel His pleasure." Both Eric and Jenny planned to be missionaries, but they disagreed about the values a missionary could hold. Jenny believed that running took Eric away from God's work. Eric was sure that God honored his values for physical fitness and competition in that phase of his life, provided he also held to his high value on religious beliefs. Eric was willing to pay a severe price for his faith, refusing to compete in the 100-yard dash in Paris because it was scheduled for Sunday morning. In the end, he won a gold medal in a different event. Eric's success in athletics later provided a platform for evangelism—others saw him as a down-to-earth Christian rather than a "holier-than-thou" missionary. Eric knew what he valued and was able to make his decisions confidently.

In the same way, recall that Pete, who no longer found his work satisfying, clarified which values mattered most to him. The process allowed him to identify a mismatch of personal and workplace values. He put to work his newfound self-awareness as he searched for opportunities in other departments and finally in other companies where his personal values were honored.

Knowing your core values can clarify your choices and help you understand which activities or settings are right for you. For instance:

- "When I realized how much I valued independence, I left a work situation where I had little influence over my own future and started my own business."
- "When I realized how important my family was to me, I restricted my job search to this region of the country."
- "With my high priority for knowledge, especially my desire to

obtain a higher academic degree, I sought employment with a company that had a tuition reimbursement program."

- "I didn't realize how important variety is to me—now I try to avoid standing committees. Instead I volunteer for one-time needs."

Knowing your priorities can help you answer questions like: *What gives my life meaning? In what ways do I influence others? What is worthwhile work for me? What deep issues of the soul will a knowledge of my values help me clarify?*

Values are one more *LifeKey* to help you understand where you can best use what God has given uniquely to you. They make clear how and where to use your spiritual gifts and life gifts. They add to your understanding of why certain vocations or service opportunities would be better choices for you. Being in charge of the children's Christmas program, for example, may fit your life gifts for creativity and management, your spiritual gifts of leadership and administration, and your passion for children's ministry—*but* if you value accuracy and control, you will be doomed to frustration as the "little lambs" wander off and the Wise Men forget to carry their gifts to the manger.

Shouldn't My Values Remain Constant?

In college, David worked as a lab technician during the day, conducting experiments on viruses that cause life-threatening illnesses. Because the studies used live viruses, the lab placed an *extremely* high value on accuracy. At night, he worked as a busboy in a restaurant. There they judged David's performance on speed—how fast he could clear tables and bus dirty dishes. The restaurant soon fired him because the day job had so conditioned him to meticulousness that he separated the silverware and neatly disposed of napkins—in short, David was the slowest busboy they had ever seen! What was of most value during the day was of little value at night.

Many of us find that daily life takes us to different arenas that applaud different sets of values. Your family may value service while your workplace values prestige. You may value tradition while the organizations to which you belong seek to change.

As you know, values from these arenas can conflict with each other. Sometimes the conflict is manageable. Sometimes the conflict is so severe that we *must* make adjustments to the situation or leave outright. And sometimes we choose to change what we value. Unlike life gifts or spiritual gifts, not all of our values are God-given, nor are they with us from birth. For example, many of us place a much higher value on religious beliefs now than we did as children. Good change! The importance of physical fitness comes and goes for most of us. If you came from a dysfunctional family, perhaps maintaining your self-respect is of utmost importance to you.

Our major values can collide when we least expect it. One family did not realize how strongly they valued loyalty until they concluded that their church no longer met the spiritual needs of their children. They firmly believed that as members they should be working to change the church, not desert it, yet they also valued passing on their faith beliefs to their children. It took several months for them to determine in this situation which values held more weight for them.

Our purpose here is not to rearrange your values but to give you a framework for viewing them clearly, for seeing how they might be conflicting in various arenas of your life, and for understanding how your values fit the roles your life calls you to play. Few individuals will ever be lucky enough to so order their lives that there are no conflicts. Most of us will always live in tension, since few of these areas are black and white. If you find yourself struggling with the ways your values conflict, you might wish to seek help with this process. Sometimes simply talking through the problems with a friend can help; in other cases you may wish to seek the help of a pastor or counselor.

Are These the Values God Wants Me to Have?

Even with no landmarks in sight, sailors of old could navigate the vast oceans simply by marking the location of the North Star and then using it to determine the direction to steer their ship. Think of your values as the North Star, always ready to provide direction as to which way to steer your life. They perhaps can form the basis for a personal mission statement. (See Writing a Personal Mission Statement, on page 241.)

The next question is whether the North Star of your values is pointing you in the direction God would have you go. As we said earlier, God's purpose is to influence your values. Search out what the Bible says about each of your top values. By using a topical Bible, for example, you might find the following verses on advancement:

> Do you see those who are skillful in their work? They will serve kings; they will not serve common people. (Proverbs 22:29, NRSV)
>
> "Whoever becomes humble like this child is the greatest in the kingdom of heaven." (Matthew 18:4, NRSV)
>
> "You are those who have stood by me in my trials; and I confer on you, just as my Father has conferred on me, a kingdom . . ." (Luke 22:28–29, NRSV)

Thus the Bible has verses that affirm honing your skills to rise as high as you can—working for kings—but it also indicates that humility and servanthood are the keys to advancement in the kingdom of God.

In the same way, you may wish to explore what the Bible has to say about things you value little, especially if you were surprised or uncomfortable at the way you prioritized them. Are you missing any values that are of paramount importance to God? Is your lack of concern for any value keeping you from the path that God would have you follow?

As we ponder our values, examining whether our lives reflect the priorities we want to hold closely, many of us sense a huge gap between who we are and who God wants us to be. We wonder if we can ever find and stick to the best path.

Paul makes it clear that mature Christians acknowledge that they are not perfect:

> Not that I have already obtained this or have already reached the goal; but I press on to make it my own, because Christ Jesus has made me his own. Beloved, I do not consider that I have made it my own; but this one thing I do: forgetting what lies behind and straining forward to what lies ahead, I press on toward the goal for the prize of the heavenly call of God in Christ Jesus. (Philippians 3:12–14, NRSV)

Paul says that this is the mature view: we are to acknowledge our shortcomings, but nevertheless let go of them so we can continue to strive toward the goal of completeness in Christ. We are to let go of discouragement and instead sense the unending forgiveness God sends our way. He loves us even though He knows we will never quite measure up.

Were you ever involved in sports? If you were, you probably had at least a few games or meets where your performance just didn't measure up to how well you did in practice. Good coaches don't tear you apart when that happens; instead, they allow you to find key factors that will help you do better the next time. God wants to help you identify the values that can be *LifeKeys* for you. In fact, God reassures you that if you take the time to let Him be your guide, He stands ready to encourage you and to help you get closer to the best path:

> He makes me lie down in green pastures,
> he leads me beside quiet waters,
> he restores my soul.
> He guides me in paths of righteousness
> for his name's sake. (Psalm 23:2–3)

Prayer

Dear God,

In this complex world, it is hard for me to know what I value, let alone what You would have me value. I understand that we need not all hold the same values, but I want so much to know Your will for me in this area. Help me listen to no one but You as I clarify what is most important to me. Show me how to work these values into the decisions I make about how to live, where to work, and how to serve You. If I find conflicts, Lord, please guide me in them. Amen.

Exercise: Clarifying Your Values

At the end of this book you will find a set of fifty-one values cards, each listing a separate value and its definition. There are some blank cards if you think of a value that we didn't include.

1. Find a place where you can lay out all of the cards.

2. Place the heading cards (*These are very valuable to me; These are valuable to me; These are not very valuable to me*) in a row at the top of your workspace.

3. Place the prompt card (*If my life were completely unencumbered, this is how I would value*_____) in a place where you can easily refer to it as you sort the cards.

4. Filling in the blank on the prompt card with each value, quickly sort the values cards into the appropriate columns, laying them out so that you can view all of the cards in one glance. Do this *rapidly*, following your feelings or instinct rather than trying to analyze each one thoroughly.

5. *Place no more than eight cards in the "These are very valuable to me" column. This could be a difficult task!*

6. Next, rank the cards within the *"These are very valuable to me"* column, placing the value that is of most importance to you at the top of that column.

7. Copy the values in the way you have sorted them onto the Values Summary (page 175). You will now have a record from which to complete the exercises.

8. Record your top eight values in LifeKeys Notations, page 239.

Values Summary

Copy the values from your values card onto this page in the order you gave to them. This will give you a working record to use for the exercises. (You need not order the second or third column, but most people find it helpful to record where they placed each value.)

These are very valuable to me	These are valuable to me	These are not very valuable to me
1. _____	1. _____	1. _____
2. _____	2. _____	2. _____
3. _____	3. _____	3. _____
4. _____	4. _____	4. _____
5. _____	5. _____	5. _____
6. _____	6. _____	6. _____
7. _____	7. _____	7. _____
8. _____	8. _____	8. _____
	9. _____	9. _____
	10. _____	10. _____
	11. _____	11. _____
	12. _____	12. _____
	13. _____	13. _____
	14. _____	14. _____
	15. _____	15. _____
	16. _____	16. _____
	17. _____	17. _____
	18. _____	18. _____
	19. _____	19. _____
	20. _____	20. _____
	21. _____	21. _____
		22. _____

Values Exercises

Listed below are seven different questions to help you work with your values. Each question indicates a common application. *Read through all of the questions. You need not do all of them, but choose two or three that are most appropriate for your current situation.*

1. **To evaluate what these values mean to you in any situation:**
   (a.) Rewrite your list of eight most important values.

   **These are very
   valuable to me**

   1. _____

   2. _____

   3. _____

   4. _____

   5. _____

   6. _____

   7. _____

   8. _____

   (b.) To the right, write your own definitions of each of these without looking at the cards. What do these values mean to you? Any thoughts about what you have written?

2. **To evaluate whether your life reflects your values:**

(a.) Pull out your calendar and think about the past week. Write out your activities below as they correspond to your top eight values.

Values   Activities

1. _____

2. _____

3. _____

4. _____

5. _____

6. _____

7. _____

8. _____

(b.) Are there one or two goals you would like to set to bring your lifestyle more in line with your values?

(c.) Which values are under your control? Where do you feel you lack control in matching your lifestyle with your values?

3. **To evaluate your current work/service environment:**
   (a.) Again, list your eight top values. Then re-sort all the cards, choosing the eight values you believe are most important in your workplace. Are there any conflicts between the two lists? (This can also be useful as a team building exercise or for family discussion.)

	Top Values	Workplace Values
1.	_____	_____
2.	_____	_____
3.	_____	_____
4.	_____	_____
5.	_____	_____
6.	_____	_____
7.	_____	_____
8.	_____	_____

   (b.) Does this explain any of the conflict or tension you feel in this setting? How might this be resolved? You may want to talk through alternatives with a trusted other.

4. **To consider whether a job or service opportunity fits your values or what atmosphere is needed to harmonize with your values:**
   Assume that you have found a job or service opportunity that fits with your life gifts, spiritual gifts, and personality type. What is the atmosphere needed for it to match with your top eight values?

5. **To consider how others perceive your values:**
   (a.) Imagine that a biographer is about to write your life story. As the writer speaks with one of your friends, a co-worker, and members of your family, what values would you like them to say you held highest?

   Friend:

   Co-worker:

   Family member:

   (b.) Are there any conflicts amongst the various viewpoints?

   (c.) What changes might you make to hold these values?

6. **To personally evaluate your own values choices:**
   Are any of your top eight values in conflict with each other? For example, valuing both financial independence and generosity can be problematic for some—or both adventure and stability! List any possible conflicts below:

7. **To discern how your values might change as you enter the next season of your life:**
   (a.) Define "next season" for yourself: new job, empty nest, end of school, retirement, whatever you believe your next stage will be:

   (b.) How do you think your values might change? Re-sort the values cards to find the top eight values for your next season.

My current top eight values	My "next season" top eight values
1. _____	_____
2. _____	_____
3. _____	_____
4. _____	_____
5. _____	_____
6. _____	_____
7. _____	_____
8. _____	_____

   (c.) Write your own definitions for any values that are new for you on this list.

(d.) What areas are under your control for making these changes? What could be difficult to control?

(e.) What areas of change will be stressful to you? What, if any, potential conflicts exist?

(f.) How does this change your priorities of God, family, work, friends? How can you maintain balance?

(g.) What two or three concrete steps can you take to move toward your "next season" values?

LifeKey 6

You are called to serve where you can harmonize with God's song in your heart!

CHAPTER 6

PASSIONS—WHAT GOD PUTS IN YOUR HEART

What's important is not how we get a dream, but whether we have one, and whether we will allow God to work in our lives so that He can accomplish what He had in mind when He gave it to us.[1]

—David Seamands

"Lyda Rose, I'm home again, Rose . . ." Was this beautiful song from *The Music Man* your introduction to barbershop music? Do you remember that the four town council members who sang it *hated* each other—until Professor Harold Hill showed them how to sing in harmony? These four had previously quibbled about everything, yet now couldn't bear to be apart, so great was their delight in their music. They sang on the courthouse steps, in the town square, in the street, and at the stable, enjoying the harmony so much that they forgot their intent to tar and feather Professor Hill.

These men had a *passion*: a desire or purpose that brought them joy, that helped them overlook their differences and difficulties, and brought its own rewards.

What Is a Passion?

Webster's defines passion as a powerful emotion: "Passion, fervor, ardor, enthusiasm, zeal." The word "enthusiasm" comes from

---

[1]David Seamands, *Living With Your Dreams* (Wheaton, Ill.: Victor Books, 1990), p. 15.

the Greek phrase *en theos*, "with God." Thus if you are *enthusiastically* pursuing a passion that God has put in your heart, you are doing it *with God*! Think of what can happen when God places these motivations in your heart.

It *is* okay for Christians to have passions, since what we are describing are *positive* passions that lead to good works, not negative, "forbidden" passions. We'd rather refer to *those* as deceptions or obsessions rather than passions. It doesn't take long to think of obsessed people with misdirected causes who brought pain to dozens, thousands, or even millions, does it? Take for example the retired minister who dreamed of a new type of airplane based on the feather design of silver geese. Assuming the dream could only have come from God, he found backers, hired engineers, and invested years of time and lots of money—only to watch the plane crash on its test flight as it failed to even get off the ground! At least we can report that no one was hurt physically because of his obsession—other examples may not be so sparing of human life and spirit.

In contrast, when you discover the passions that God has in mind for you, you can operate with enthusiasm, "with God."

Positive Passions in Action

It happened to Nehemiah, who was just one of the thousands of Jewish exiles living in Babylon. When Nehemiah heard that Jerusalem still lay in ruins, he fasted, wept, and prayed for several days—and then took action. He gained permission from his captors to lead a party back to Jerusalem to rebuild the city walls. Once there he formulated his plan:

> I set out during the night with a few men. I had not told anyone *what my God had put in my heart* to do for Jerusalem. (Nehemiah 2:12, *emphasis ours*)

The rest of the story is full of drama. The workers hauled stone with one hand while holding their swords in the other to fend off attackers. They worked by day and stood guard over their progress at night. Conspirators hired false prophets to discredit Nehemiah, but the walls were rebuilt in just fifty-two days! Through it all, Nehemiah was convinced that he was *en theos*, carrying out God's designs.

Of course, few of us are called on to rebuild a city, but what might God put in your heart today?

Marlys could be considered a modern-day Nehemiah, although she would probably deny it. Marlys knew that God loved her. She experienced that love during the awful time after her husband had deserted her, through the long years of single parenting, and in the midst of many other events in her life. Along with teaching school and being a grandmother, Marlys constantly searched for ways to live out her passion to serve others so they could experience God's love as well.

When her friend Sophie phoned her to explain a new refugee outreach project, Marlys willingly agreed to meet to hear more. Sophie told her, "The refugees in this camp have nothing but the clothes they were wearing when the armies approached their villages. One of our missionaries invited each family to write a letter that detailed their needs. I suppose we could just ship food and clothing in bulk, but I would love to answer the letters personally and send each family a box prepared *just* for them."

"How many families are there?" Marlys asked as she gazed at the photos the missionary had taken of the tents, the dirty stream that was the camp's only water supply, and the children dressed in ragged clothing.

"We have letters from twelve hundred families. Two of the teachers at my school started translating them from Spanish. The women's group at my church held a clothing drive that took care of one-third of the families' needs. With two-thirds more to go, I'm talking with other churches and people like you to help out with the rest. We need to respond as soon as possible—the letters are already a few months old."

Seeing the photos and hearing about the plight of these families, Marlys acted with enthusiasm on her passion for serving others. She didn't hesitate but a moment. "Give me four hundred of the letters. I know a few people who speak Spanish. . . ."

"Some of the families have a dozen children," warned Sophie.

"Oh, I won't try to do this alone."

Distributing flyers and then collecting clothing in her own neighborhood produced enough to make Marlys's small basement look like an overstocked thrift store. When her grown children saw her efforts and her needs, they quickly canvassed their own neighborhoods. Her granddaughters convinced a group of teenage friends to spend an entire Saturday cleaning and sorting toys as well as packing the boxes to be shipped. With the help of her prayer group, friends, and neighbors whose curiosity was aroused, Marlys's basement soon became a temporary storehouse for four hundred neatly packed, individually labeled boxes of love.

Marlys called Sophie and happily reported, "The boxes are ready to go. Does that take care of all the letters, or can I do more?" If there was more to do, she was ready to start again with enthusiasm, knowing she was acting "with God."

How Did They Know What God Had in Mind?

In building the walls of a city or preparing a shipment of boxes to refugees, both Nehemiah and Marlys were ready to act on what God put into their heart. But how did they know what God had in mind for them?

1. They were already in a relationship with God.
God's will is intricately tied to who He is. Many people who start down this path of discovering their passions focus too heavily on trying to discern God's will rather than on trying to get to know God. Note that we are called human *beings,* not human *doings!* So many of us have been judged all of our lives by what we *do* that it is hard for us to imagine a God who wants us to *be,* who wants us to know Him better so He can make a home within us.

Jesus called himself the vine and us His branches. Branches need time to grow strong before they can bear fruit. In the meantime, branches are called to "abide," to wait while remaining in the same place. When we are ready, God can guide us in bearing fruit. In addition, God can more easily convey passions to those who already are familiar with how He works. Do you need to know God better?

2. They were able to recognize God at work.
Both Marlys and Nehemiah were actively asking God to show them how they could serve, looking for ways to be His hands for others. Hearing God's voice, however, is seldom easy for anyone—Paul, writing to the Corinthian church, spoke of seeing now only dimly, as through a mirror. Waiting for "clear direction" can be dangerous. Even when God gives it, people often misunderstand! As a boy, the prophet Samuel didn't recognize God's voice calling

him in the night (1 Samuel 3). His master, Eli, identified the voice as God's.

We all struggle today with hearing God's voice. One father was torn between wanting to serve on a mission trip and being reluctant to take an entire week of vacation away from his family. As he was debating what he should do, his boss called him in and said, "You've been working too hard—take an extra week off this year." (Have you *ever* heard of that happening?) He *still* wasn't sure if he should go on the mission trip. Most of us go through seasons of our lives without a clue about which way to turn. Yet we are promised,

> Do not conform any longer to the pattern of this world, but be transformed by the renewing of your mind. Then you will be able to test and approve what God's will is—his good, pleasing and perfect will. (Romans 12:2)

God's revelations to you have a pattern: first comes discovering who God is, then growing in maturity and fruit, and finally, discerning His will.

3. *They already understood how God could use their gifts; they didn't have to stop to analyze the fit.*

When a passion hits, it is only people who have honestly taken stock of their own abilities—not in false pride or in false humility—who instantly know what to do. One of our motivations for *LifeKeys* is to help people reach the point that they can recognize their passions—but they first need to explore what they are capable of doing.

In a recent survey, George Barna asked American adults whether they knew of their spiritual gifts.[2] Of those who had heard of spiritual gifts, fewer than a third could correctly name even one gift. Less than a quarter could name a single one of their own spiritual gifts. No wonder it is hard to dream! That is why we ask you to consider your passions only after you understand your other *LifeKeys*. Now that you have discovered the unique ways God has gifted you, it should be easier for you to find those places to serve that have your name written all over them!

As you take the time to develop your relationship with God,

---

[2]News Release, Barna Research Group, Ltd., Glendale, Calif. "Most Christians Are Oblivious to Their Spiritual Gifts" (October 3, 1995).

He calls you into servanthood—to know what you are capable of doing and then to be a good steward of how He has gifted you.

Even with the motivation that their passions provided, however, neither Nehemiah nor Marlys faced an easy task. Both spent a great deal of time praying, gathering information, locating resources, and planning how they and others could best accomplish the work.

How Do I Find My Passions?

We hope that by now you have a basic understanding of your life gifts and spiritual gifts, as well as how your personality and values affect the atmosphere in which you would most likely choose to use them. The remaining big question is to discern which specific tasks, projects, or causes hold for you the most pull or energy. Where, in other words, can you be *en theos*—enthusiastic—with God?

There are as many answers as there are people. The answers might come easily to you. Are your shelves filled with books on gardening? Do seed catalogs flood your mailbox while you wait for those warm days to be able to dig the soil and start your garden? Before you say, "Well, gardening isn't a God-given passion," think of the places where God could use a good gardener. Perhaps an elderly neighbor longs for help with her window boxes. Or your church's landscaping needs attention. Or a sick individual's spirits could be lifted with flowers from your garden.

What if new product development and marketing holds your interest? When you're working on a fresh idea, hours go by in between glances at your watch. You eagerly make and return phone calls in hopes of finding prospective users because you know they will benefit from your product. Besides, a successful product creates more jobs. If this is you, your passions for developing and marketing new things may tie in with God's needs for recruiting and promoting. From helping others to see how they can benefit by teaching Sunday school to promoting educational opportunities, God could put many things in your heart.

Passions come in all colors, shapes, and sizes—one size definitely does *not* fit all. Your passions may be as focused as the prayer group that works together to ensure that a shelter for abused women and their children has an ample supply of new or gently used toys. Or your passions may be as broad as the community organization that works to prevent abuse and fund that shelter.

You may be given what is *in the eyes of the world* a small passion, like maintaining a pickup basketball court in the churchyard so that neighborhood kids feel welcomed by the church. Know that *in God's eyes* no passion is small. Or you may be one given a passion that targets thousands, such as ending gang wars in a city. God asks some of us to help one person at a time, others to marshal support for widespread efforts. It isn't the size of your passion that counts, but whether or not it is from God. The world can use all kinds of help.

If you aren't a dreamer—someone who easily thinks of ways to be *en theos*—there are some helpful paths to discovering what is or might become a passion for you:

- *Are you a "one-passion" person?*

  Are you an "I'm pretty happy anytime I'm building (cooking, running, driving)" person? Your passions may center on a specific life gift or interest, be it teaching, singing, accounting, or backpacking. Your path to enthusiasm may be finding different arenas that need your skills.

  This doesn't mean you have to accept every offer that comes your way. For example, one person with a love for cooking and the gift of administration organized church dinners out of a passion to increase fellowship in the church. Another with the same gifts organized delivery of meals to a family in crisis out of a passion to help those who grieve. Same gifts, different passions. Note that neither of them felt called, that is, felt enthusiasm, to fill the role of the other!

- *Are you a "make me an offer" person?*

  Would you like some options or a chance to try something before signing up? If you are asked, "What excites you?" does your mind project a blank screen? Or are you so busy in this season of life that you cringe at the thought of scrambling to envision your passion?

  You may enjoy linking up with visionaries—people who have the idea, plan, and passion for a given service—who need more help to make their vision a reality. This book is an example of "make me an offer" passions—when David conveyed his vision for the class, Jane and Sandra, who had never considered developing a church class on people's giftedness, thought, "I have some life gifts that could be useful here!" We accepted David's "make me an offer."

Sandra, already involved in helping others find places or positions that were a good fit, had longed to add a spiritual dimension to her efforts. The class augmented an existing passion. Jane, with a lifelong interest in helping others find the joy in service, signed on because she thought her consulting skills could be applied to improving the use of class time, and she soon found her passion for writing put to use as well.

Frequently the "make me an offer" folk become very passionate about the project as well. (Here we are—Jane, David, and Sandra—still working with *LifeKeys* years later!) If you try a few offers or come up with some yourself, God can begin to direct you and guide you into areas where you will find great excitement.

- *Are your passions right under your nose?*

What about the heartfelt desire to be the best parent/friend/employee you can be? The most considerate neighbor? A compassionate coach? A teacher who makes a difference in the lives of those entrusted to him or her? You may not need to look any further than your current activities to uncover your passions.

One man changed the atmosphere in his office simply by taking the first reconciling step of having lunch with the three co-workers he liked least. When he showed that he cared, they passed the same kindness on to others. In an amazingly short space of time his office changed from a hostile, backbiting organization to a place of camaraderie.

Note that God can put passions into our heart in any arena, not just in the Church or with the disenfranchised or through outreach programs. One of the early participants in a *LifeKeys* class at our church said, "I've always had a passion for politics, but I've never made room for it—until now!" He became intensely active in the grassroots efforts of his political party, trying to bring the values of his faith to that arena.

To sum up, in many instances people don't need to search very hard to find a passion they can act on *en theos*—with God. Start by reviewing what you have already discovered about yourself through your life gifts, spiritual gifts, personality type, and values. Then ask God to begin to guide you from where you are to where you can work with Him.

"But My Plate Is Too Full to Add Passions!"

If you find yourself a bit reluctant to *even begin* looking for passions, knowing full well that your life is too busy as it is, believe us, you have a lot of company! While it is true that Jesus compelled us to feed the hungry, welcome strangers, clothe the needy, care for the sick, and visit those in prison,[3] you may not be in a stage of your life where you can do all of those at once!

The Bible is full of people who waited a *long* time for their chance to act. Jesus was about thirty when he began His ministry. After his conversion, Paul spent ten or so years in a small town before beginning his missionary travels. David is described as a youth when Samuel anointed him king; he was thirty before he finally became king of all Israel.

Or consider Esther. She concealed her Jewish background when she was chosen as a possible wife for the king of Babylon. When it became apparent that she alone might be able to influence the king to change his decree that all Jews be killed, her uncle Mordecai told her, "Who knows? Perhaps you have come to royal dignity for just such a time as this."[4] Who knows for what purposes God might be preparing you?

If this is a season of waiting, consider what you can do to ready yourself for the next season. Do you need a deeper understanding of Scripture, better organizational skills, or a network of people who have done similar things? Would computer classes help? Should you be saving money for a van to use in future ministry? Are there ways that your family could join you in your passion, thereby allowing your family to be *en theos* together?

Finally, God has places for you to be *en theos* no matter what your schedule. Look for ways to serve where you are. Some ideas:

- If your house is constantly overrun by neighborhood children,

---

[3]Matthew 25:35–36.
[4]Esther 4:14, NRSV.

could your passion be teaching children how to be kind to one another?

- If the politics of your office are destructive to some, could your passion be building good relationships among your fellow employees?
- If you are busy all day long, could your passion be to act as a kind and considerate person toward each customer/friend/relative you meet?

If you don't see yourself as a dreamer, a one-talent person, or in any of our other scenarios, perhaps God is giving you this time to deepen your relationship with Him in preparation for those passions yet to come. Use this time to grow in your trust for Him. If God gives you a passion, are you willing to step out in faith? Be able to answer that question with a "Yes, of course!" Believe that God loves you enough to place the right passions in your heart.

So often, though, as we try to get to know God better, we misunderstand the way He calls us into service. Remember the story of the ten talents? A rich man gave five talents to one servant, who traded and earned five more. A second servant was given two talents, which he doubled as well. To these servants the master said, "Well done. You have been trustworthy in a few things; I will put you in charge of many things."

A third servant, given just one talent, hid it away for fear of losing it, for he understood his master to be harsh. When the master found out that this last servant hadn't even bothered to put it in the ancient equivalent of an insured interest-bearing account, he became angry at the servant's overcaution. The master then took from the servant the one talent and gave it to the servant with the ten talents (Matthew 25:14–29).

The tragedy of the third servant is that he misunderstood. He hid his talent away because he was convinced his master was harsh rather than benevolent. Are you guilty of thinking the same of God? God doesn't stand ready at any moment to zap us for erring while trying to use our gifts. Rather, this parable suggests we sadden Him when we are afraid to try.

We are not to worry about how capable we are—we are simply to make the most of whatever we have. We have all been given a special package of gifts to use for God's glory. Trust Him and see what He can do with you. Someday you too will hear the words, "Well done, good and faithful servant."

"Can Passions Change?"

It is okay for passions to change as your life changes. A person who just entered the business world may no longer have the passion to lead the Bible study that was so rewarding while in college; the old passion may be replaced with a burning new desire to be a responsible employee with godly principles. Similarly, a couple with young children may need to take a break from working with the church youth group; the desire to lay their own foundation for good parenting could fill their hearts. Or a person experiencing illness or a life crisis may need to concentrate on renewing his or her own spiritual resources first; the desire to grow in faith in order to serve better in the future may be a person's most urgent God-given passion during a time of recovery.

Occasionally God calls for a complete redirection of our passions. One much-in-demand evangelist was booked up to four years in advance. When his high school son started to neglect schoolwork and in general cause his parents worry, the evangelist canceled *all four years* of engagements. His passions refocused to include more time with his family, and together they moved hundreds of miles away so the evangelist father could take a job with a parish church. The son, who quickly settled down again once his father was close at hand, went on to establish his own ministry of evangelism that grew to reach many more people than his father had! Neither passion pursued by the father was better; both were just different ways of serving God.

Sometimes God even changes your passions in ways that don't seem very *en theos* to you or to those around you, but life can prove to be surprising. One banker who retired because of health problems confided to a friend that he had always wanted to be a disc jockey. The friend knew the head of a Christian radio station who made a deal with the banker: "You can have a go at being a DJ if you'll take over as my financial manager." While the banker found he lacked the necessary life gifts to succeed on the air, he became a vital part of the station's management team!

How Can I Know If a Passion Is Right for Me?

As you contemplate what your passions might be, you may wonder how you can be sure a passion is from God and not an obsession flowing from some other source.

Even on a small scale, passions need to be tested. One couple with a special-needs child volunteered to work with a church committee to reach out to other families with special-needs children. The couple seemed genuinely interested in helping others, but the pastor was uneasy with their participation. Through her counsel, the couple realized that they were still too bitter about their own situation to work well with other families. The minister helped them find a different ministry where they were better able to use their gifts.

Test your passions in the same way you test other decisions:

- Would Scripture prohibit me from acting on this passion?
- Do those who understand my gifts and talents believe I would be effective exercising this passion?
- Do the trusted people around me see this passion as a possibility grounded in reality? As we discuss this below, note, however, that sometimes God enables us to stretch beyond our "normal" capabilities!
- How well do I understand my motives? Could they possibly be *too* self-serving?
- As I pursue this passion, does my motivation increase or decrease the more I work with it?

There Is NO WAY I Have All of the Gifts Needed for This Passion

If you feel as though you don't have what it takes to follow through on what God has put in your heart, there are two things to keep in mind:

- Sometimes God works with a person, for a time, in a new, more focused and powerful way to carry out His purposes. For example, before Saul was made king, Samuel revealed to him, "The Spirit of the Lord will come upon you in power, and you will prophesy with them; and you will be changed into a different person. Once these are fulfilled, do whatever your hand finds to do, for God is with you" (1 Samuel 10:6–7).
- Sometimes the gifts that are needed are in the people around you. Marlys didn't pack all of those boxes or translate all of the letters herself. Nehemiah didn't build the walls single-hand-

edly. Even if you are missing abilities that you believe are crucial, start to share your dreams with others, asking God to let them know if they are to join in. If you become convinced through the discerning questions above that a passion *is* from God, seek guidance as to how to carry on with it, whether or not you can do it alone.

Keep Searching

One of the biggest dangers in this whole process of looking for passions is *analysis paralysis*, becoming so worried over discovering just what God has in mind for you that you never get around to *any* passions. We suggest that you start with examining how God has designed you. Add in where you see God at work, and you can't be too far from the place God has in mind for you. Don't become paralyzed by looking for only one "right" spot to serve. Many, many passions start as small inklings. It isn't until you're in the middle of the *en theos* experience that you know the breadth of what God has planned.

One woman was hesitant to lead a new support group, and did so only when a friend agreed to co-lead with her. The woman soon discovered that she had the spiritual gift of *shepherding* and found her leadership role very natural, very *en theos*. If at the beginning God had let her see her future role as the organizer and leader of an entire small group ministry at another church, she probably would have said, "Sorry, God, wrong person." Because she had trusted God enough to take that first step, God was able to work through her.

Henry Blackaby puts it this way:

> "What is God's will for my life?" is not the best question to ask. I think the right question is simply, "What is God's will?" Once I know God's will, then I can adjust my life to Him and His purposes.[5]

Remember Marlys as she was *en theos* with her passion to help others? She trusted God, she knew her own gifts, she saw God at work, and she signed up to help! Discovering what God has put

---

[5]Henry T. Blackaby and Claude V. King, *Experiencing God* (Nashville: Broadman and Holman Publishers, 1994), p. 18. All rights reserved. Used by permission.

in your heart—what your passions are—can bring the greatest contentment imaginable. Picture God waiting to put a new song in your heart, a song that comes from acting upon the passions that He designed just for you.

Prayer

Dear God,

I want to serve en theos, *with You, but this is unknown territory. Help me remember that discovering what You have put in my heart can bring me the greatest contentment possible. You do not call all of us to be leaders or to care for children or to go to the mission field, but instead You call each of us to the tasks for which You designed us. Be my guide as I work to uncover my passions. Amen.*

What Can I Do *En Theos,* With God?

We talked about four different approaches to discovering passions. Think about which approach might best suit you and turn first to the questions below for that approach:

- **The "One-Talent" approach**—those people who look for chances to use a specific life gift or spiritual gift in a variety of arenas where they can become *en theos,* with God.
- **The "Make Me an Offer" approach**—those people who know their life gifts and spiritual gifts and are excited about teaming up with leaders who have a vision for new or existing ministries.
- **The "Right Under Your Nose" approach**—those people who might act on passions right where they are.
- **The "Dreamer" approach**—those people who find this process easy and exciting and are ready to simply dream about what they might do for God.

Take the next few days to begin to answer these questions. Realize that many passions develop over a period of time. (Remember, we are allowed time to abide as we learn more about God and His plans.) If this is your first experience in discerning what you might do for God, give yourself *ample* time!

And, we suggest that you not try to answer all of the questions, even in the section that suits you best. It is better if you start with one or two questions in the section you choose rather than trying to answer all of the questions at once—unless you are *highly* motivated!

For the "One Talent" People

1. From Chapters 2 and 3, list the life gifts and spiritual gifts you identified as your own. Which of these could you use *en theos,* with God?

2. The following list is meant to trigger your own thoughts. It is

by no means exhaustive or all-inclusive. Try hard to think of *other* areas! Which skills might you enjoy using?

- ☐ Artistic expressions
- ☐ Car repair
- ☐ Carpentry
- ☐ Coaching athletics
- ☐ Computers
- ☐ Cooking/entertaining
- ☐ Crafts
- ☐ Driving
- ☐ Financial planning/ budgets
- ☐ Foreign languages
- ☐ Gardening
- ☐ General management
- ☐ Graphic arts
- ☐ Home repair
- ☐ Interior design
- ☐ Investigating
- ☐ Mathematics
- ☐ Office administration
- ☐ Organizing events/parties
- ☐ Photography
- ☐ Political pursuits
- ☐ Reading
- ☐ Research
- ☐ Sewing
- ☐ Speaking
- ☐ Storytelling
- ☐ Teaching
- ☐ Time management
- ☐ Word processing

What other areas can you add?

3. Which of these can you most easily relate to or reach out to?

- ☐ Abuse victims
- ☐ Adults
- ☐ Business and professional men
- ☐ Business and professional women
- ☐ Children
- ☐ Community neighbors
- ☐ Couples
- ☐ Disabled or sick people
- ☐ Elderly
- ☐ Ethnic groups/refugees
- ☐ Infants
- ☐ International students
- ☐ Members of dysfunctional families
- ☐ Missionaries
- ☐ Newlyweds
- ☐ New church members
- ☐ Parents of young children
- ☐ Singles
- ☐ Substance abusers
- ☐ Teens
- ☐ Unemployed
- ☐ Young adults

Other people you could work with or partner with are:

4. Looking at your own life, which activities do you truly enjoy?

For the "Make Me an Offer" People

1. In the space below, write down the passions or interests of people you know who are already *en theos*. How could you help them accomplish their dreams? (Remember, sometimes the project may not be as important to you as the character of the person in charge.)

2. Find out what ministries and missions your church actively supports. Which of these interest you?

3. Get a listing of the most recent volunteer opportunities available at your church or at another ministry that seems appealing to you. Review these and write down which tasks interest you. If there is a volunteer notebook (one with descriptions of available opportunities), take time to review it for ideas.

4. Contact the formal or informal leadership of your spiritual

community in areas that seem attractive to you (for example, adult education, outreach, member involvement, music, etc.). Find out their volunteer needs.

For the "Right Under Your Nose" People

1. In your current life circumstances, what passions could become your focus (for example: parenting, workplace issues, grief support):
2. With the issues listed below, where could you help right now?

☐ Addictions
☐ Divorce
☐ Education (or tutoring)
☐ Employment issues
☐ Finance/budget problems
☐ Health problems
☐ Housing needs
☐ Legal advice/concerns

☐ Maintenance or repair needs
☐ Marital problems
☐ Parenting
☐ Personal relationships
☐ Physical disabilities
☐ Spiritual problems
☐ Terminal illnesses

Other:

3. What places are easy for you to serve in this season of your life? What activities do you already take part in that could offer further opportunities for service that you would enjoy?

4. As you look through your life gifts and spiritual gifts, how could you expand using them, finding ways to minister to others?

For the "Dreamers"

1. If you had no fear of failure and limitless time and resources at your disposal, what would you do?

2. If you could do some of the things you either feel you *should* do or have *wanted* to do for a long time, what would these be?

3. Name three people who have accomplished something that you would like to do:

Name   Accomplishment

(a.)

(b.)

(c.)

Because of their example, what might you think of trying?

(a.)

(b.)

(c.)

4. Who is the one person who has made the strongest positive impact on your life? Why do you believe that person had such a powerful influence on you?

As a result of their influence, where might you like to invest your time and effort?

After completing these questions, summarize here what you have found.

In a few sentences, try to summarize two or three possible passions you believe God may have put in your heart, places of service where you could act *en theos*:

Choose one of those possible passions and state as specifically as possible how you might carry it out in action.

LifeKey 7

Keep in step with God's syncopation for YOUR life.

CHAPTER 7

LIFE CHOICES—ORCHESTRATING YOUR PRIORITIES

Time is significant because it is so rare. It is completely irretrievable. You can never repeat it or relive it. There is no such thing as a literal instant replay. That appears only on film. It travels alongside us every day, yet it has eternity wrapped up in it.[1]

—Charles R. Swindoll

By now you've read the bulk of this book—and done a great deal of discovery and reflection. We hope that with each chapter the nature of who you are—your life gifts, spiritual gifts, personality type, values, and passions—has become increasingly clear. Completing the passions exercise may even have enabled you to envision an exciting area of service or ministry that seems to fit perfectly and you would love to begin. Ready, set, stop!

Stop, you say? Yes! Here's why. People who work through these materials with us often bewail, "It may be exciting to understand my life gifts and spiritual gifts, but how can I possibly find time to use them for God's purposes?"

"I'm already working two jobs just to pay off college debts and keep my apartment."

"I don't have enough time for the kids as it is."

"I haven't even taken a vacation in two years."

LifeKeys tells you who you are and what you do best—intensely useful information. You can use it to come to peace with how God has designed you and possibly to better understand how He designed those close to you. It will help you sharpen your job skills, discover new leisure activities, and find meaningful points of service in your church and community. Nevertheless, all this information will do you no long-term, real-life good if *time constraints* keep you from putting it into action. So as we move toward a complete picture of orchestrating a life of harmony, let's take a look at time and busyness.

We know deep within us that the world is an incredibly busy place—and that our busyness is only getting worse. It wasn't long ago that futurists were predicting that the advent of computers would shorten the average work week. Instead, people find that on top of the forty-plus hours they work they can continue to be "at work" via cellular phones and laptop PC's. The virtual office of modern technology compels people to take their jobs wherever they go. And go they do—if not physically, then through fax and e-mail. We can close a deal or answer inquiries twenty-four hours a day with instantaneous worldwide communication.

On the home front, the latest labor-saving devices simply raised the standards, as if being a parent weren't enough. Home-baked bread? Sure. Crisply ironed laundry? Sure. Perfectly manicured lawns? Why not? We all *expect* to accomplish more in less time, but instead we wind up with *no* time. A chance to redirect? Use our gifts for God? Maybe that's okay for others, you think, or maybe after I retire. . . .

Even God took the seventh day to rest, yet people think they can get by without a lull in their schedule! With everything open on Sundays, we face a smorgasbord of *productive* activities. Because we can now do our work seven days a week, many of us lose the respite the Sabbath was meant to provide. Why relax? Why refocus on God? By filling up each day of the week, we often lose perspective on the whole of our lives. Gone is a weekly, ever-repeating opportunity to reflect and to reorient our direction. Schedules so dictate our lives that we forget we can choose to change.

Is this hectic pace really the life Jesus had in mind for us when He promised, "I came that they may have life, and have it abundantly?"[2]

---

[2]John 10:10, RSV.

We are well aware that you can attend lengthy seminars, read books, and buy day-planners to learn how to manage your time. Our objective is not an alternative time-management system—instead, we hope to help you consciously examine your life choices. It is interesting to note that some of today's best-selling time-management systems help you work to focus priorities so you can better manage your time, thus allowing you to experience a life of meaningful purpose. We hope that *LifeKeys* is encouraging you to do the same.

Our goal in this chapter is to look at what we call "life choices" to provide a biblical perspective on the decisions you face and give you a chance to reflect on where your time goes. Do your values match how you use your time? Is your time flexible enough to allow yourself to align with God's purposes? Are your current life choices your enemy or your ally?

God's Time

> . . . *God made us plain and simple, but we have made ourselves very complicated.* (Ecclesiastes 7:29, TEV)

If you were given a three-year assignment of designing and implementing a task force to evangelize the world—without using television, newspapers, or radio—how would you begin? Form a committee to design a mission statement? Put together a business plan? Assemble a team of experts? Pinpoint all the critical events and strategize how to head off problems?

This, of course, was the goal of Jesus, but how did He choose to reach it?

Jesus had a strategic plan to carry out this assignment, but it contained few of the elements we consider so necessary to successful planning. If we look at what He did, we can begin to see the choices God would have us make. Here is what we see:

1. Put first things first—seek the Kingdom of God.

> As Jesus and his disciples were on their way, he came to a village where a woman named Martha opened her home to him. She had a sister called Mary, who sat at the Lord's feet listening to what he said. But Martha was distracted by all the

preparations that had to be made. She came to him and asked, "Lord, don't you care that my sister has left me to do the work by myself? Tell her to help me!"

"Martha, Martha," the Lord answered, "you are worried and upset about many things, but only one thing is needed. Mary has chosen what is better, and it will not be taken away from her." (Luke 10:38–42)

What does this passage mean? That we should all devote our lives to worship and study? Perhaps a few of us are meant to, but if no one cooked or farmed or nurtured children, life on earth would soon cease to be! Jesus fully expected to receive a meal at Martha's house.

Martha, however, placed the task of meal preparation before her relationship with Jesus. We often do the same, hoping to squeeze God in between deadlines and phone calls. What Jesus is saying is that God desires us to have a relationship with Him. This relationship would appear to benefit us far more than it does God, yet as we can see from the story of Mary and Martha, He clearly insists on closeness, that we deepen our reliance on Him.

God's intent is not that you go through rote, ordered gestures, but that you find a way to escape life's distractions in order to spend time with Him. *LifeKeys* stresses each person's uniqueness; included in that uniqueness is the premise that there is more than one way to be in an ongoing relationship with God. If you read through the descriptions of each personality type (pages 138–153), it is obvious that making room for God can be done in a variety of ways. You may or may not, for example, benefit from a daily time of quiet prayer and study to the extent another person would.

For some people, meaningful time with God may come *best* through bringing to mind a certain verse of Scripture throughout the day. Others may focus their thoughts on God during a daily walk or during a long period of quiet only once or twice a week. Still others find that music or dance turns their thoughts to the Creator.

Talk with others about what has worked for them. Try different approaches. Consider working with a spiritual director to enrich this part of your life. Above all, remember what Jesus told Martha: "Only one thing is needed."

As you schedule your days keep asking yourself, "What is really required today? Have I made room for the *one thing* that is really needed in the midst of the urgent demands of life?" God is waiting for you to listen to Him. Seek time with God first as you work to make life choices.

2. Know your mission.

Jesus knew His mission—what He was called to Earth to do. In Capernaum, news had spread of His miracles:

> That evening after sunset the people brought to Jesus all the sick and demon-possessed. The whole town gathered at the door, and Jesus healed many who had various diseases. He also drove out many demons, but he would not let the demons speak because they knew who he was.
>
> Very early in the morning, while it was still dark, Jesus got up, left the house and went off to a solitary place, where he prayed. Simon and his companions went to look for him, and when they found him, they exclaimed: "Everyone is looking for you!"
>
> Jesus replied, "Let us go somewhere else—to the nearby villages—so I can preach there also. That is why I have come." So he traveled throughout Galilee, preaching in their synagogues and driving out demons. (Mark 1:32–39)

Jesus knew that His mission was to spread the news about the Kingdom of God. That meant that once people had heard His teachings and had witnessed His healings, He moved on.

Have *you* identified *your* mission? Usually there are many places to live out your mission: your mission as a spouse or parent or child, as a Christian, as a neighbor, as an employee, as a friend. Knowing your mission and taking it seriously will help determine your priorities.

The process of this book—identifying your life gifts, spiritual gifts, personality type, values, and passions—provides the tools you need to craft a mission statement for your life. If you are ready, you can use the questions in Writing a Personal Mission Statement (p. 241) to guide you through this process.

A well-defined mission statement spells out your priorities in a way that leads you to say "Yes!" to activities and requests from others that are right for you. As a member of our church put it,

"I ask myself this: Given my mission, is this a *good* choice for me or an *excellent* choice? It's best to leave the good choices for others—the excellent ones are all I can handle." She finds that knowing her mission keeps her focused on her priorities.

Priorities are funny. Even if you know something is of utmost importance, you will not get to it unless you consciously make time for it. Urgent events (phone calls, pushy folks, deadlines made by others) tend to keep you from the important. In Capernaum, there were plenty of urgent things for Jesus to do. Surely the people there could have kept Jesus busy with healings, debates, and teachings for weeks on end. Had Jesus not been acutely aware of the life choices embodied in His mission, He might have been tempted to take up residence in just one place that needed and accepted Him. Instead, His mission and priorities led Him to move on.

Consistently having time and energy for your top priorities means you will have to:

- *Know what they are.* (For help with this, go back to the values exercises and review your priorities in each area of your life.)
- *Look ahead.* Plan monthly or even seasonally, not just daily and weekly. What are your busy times? Where can you make room for your priorities in the midst of the urgent? Without scheduling in advance, you might miss your children's activities or other important family time. You won't easily find time for friends. You are unlikely to have time for planning a service project or taking part in a ministry unless you firmly plant these events on your calendar. And you also need time for *no* schedule—times each month, week, and day that allow you to live spontaneously. Search out how full your calendar should be by reviewing the Judging/Perceiving preferences you identified in Chapter 4. What works best for you?
- *Learn to say "No" to the* unimportant *urgent and postpone the* perceived *urgent.* Look for patterns in the events or activities that interrupt you or keep you from your priorities. A writer of historical fiction, for example, discovered a pattern of too many phone calls—each of which pulled her mind back to the present and away from the time period of her story. Her solution was an answering machine and a set time each day for returning calls. A minister had to learn to evaluate people's requests to determine if they were as urgent as everyone said and

if he was the only one who could respond. Perhaps a request can wait until you have more time in your schedule. Maybe you need to say "No" or offer to find someone else to help out.

3. Know your limits.

In Mark 6:32 we see Jesus attempt to take His disciples to a quiet place for rest after their first preaching tour. The crowds spotted Jesus and followed Him to the remote area He had chosen for prayer. Rather than avoid the crowds, Jesus had compassion on them and willingly taught for the rest of the day. At dinnertime, the disciples wanted to send the crowds away, but instead Jesus fed them through the miracle of the five loaves of bread and two fish. Read what happened when the people had finished eating:

> Immediately Jesus made his disciples get into the boat and go on ahead of him to Bethsaida, while he dismissed the crowd. After leaving them, he went into the hills to pray. (Mark 6:45–46)

Jesus knew when He and the disciples could handle no more. He understood that only if we find time to rest can we meet the spiritual, mental, and physical demands of life. Yes, people came first, but only after the work of replenishing the spirit.

Look at the word "recreation." You need to re-*create* yourself through activities that bring rest to your body, mind, and soul. You may be re-created through time with a book, a long hike, or a cup of tea with a good friend. Review your life gifts, those areas that are of interest to you, to see what might be helpful to allow you a place or activity to replenish.

Do you make *time* for any re-creation activities such as those suggested by your particular life gifts profile? If you seldom find such time, ponder how you might alter your life choice to nourish yourself so that you can truly nourish others. Taking good care of yourself *must* be one of life's priorities. Without this care, you may fall victim to the many health problems related to stress. When you don't respect yourself and your limits, you lessen your ability to be a truly present help for others. Besides, stressed-out people are crabby, ineffective people who are seldom good company.

So then, a Sabbath rest still remains for the people of God;

for those who enter God's rest also cease from their labors as God did from his. Let us therefore make every effort to enter that rest, so that no one may fall through such disobedience as theirs. (Hebrews 4:9–11, NRSV)

4. *Simplify your life.*

Look at the birds of the air; they neither sow nor reap nor gather into barns, and yet your heavenly Father feeds them. Are you not of more value than they? And can any of you by worrying add a single hour to your span of life? And why do you worry about clothing? Consider the lilies of the field, how they grow; they neither toil nor spin, yet I tell you, even Solomon in all his glory was not clothed like one of these. But if God so clothes the grass of the field, which is alive today and tomorrow is thrown into the oven, will he not much more clothe you—you of little faith? (Matthew 6:26–30, NRSV)

Do you ever look at your possessions as time-takers? You shop for them, pay for them, learn to use them, store them, clean them, keep them from being stolen, organize them . . . How many of you know how to program the VCR you purchased to free you from the tyranny of TV schedules? How many of you avoid using your time-saving food processor because it takes too long to wash it and put it away?

Think of your schedule or your family's schedule. Are there things that you do only because you *always* have or think you *should*? Perhaps no one would mind cutting a few courses from Christmas dinner if doing so freed the hosts to spend more time talking to and otherwise relating with their guests. Maybe now is the time to check with family and friends to see if the "traditions" are still as restoring and energizing to everyone as they once were.

God tells us not to worry about our lives—what we shall eat or drink, or what we will wear. It's a directive to seek a *simpler* life! Jesus let God's principles guide Him. Jesus therefore had most of the hours of His day available for ministry. The Bible, however, does not instruct *all* of us to sell *all* of our possessions in order to simplify our lives. The book of Acts mentions several early Christians who kept their homes, using them along with their wealth or earnings to help the Church. The early Christians still had possessions, but they were willing to share them. The point is to hold material things lightly, to keep priorities straight, and to not let your daily tasks and possessions *own* you.

No one can define simplicity for you since one person's simplicity is another person's nightmare.[3] Buying the cheapest model of bike is not simplicity if long-distance cycling is your means of reducing stress. Choosing secondhand clothes is not simplicity if you feel scruffy or do it only to appear thrifty. And driving a car to its bitter end is only simplicity if the vehicle still safely and reliably meets your needs. Any attempt to define simplicity for someone else can quickly deteriorate into legalism. Our point here is this: take a look at what you have and how you spend your time and see what things keep you from your priorities. If necessary, simplify.

Simplicity brings a powerful freedom to live as God wants you to live. In his book *Celebration of Discipline*, Richard Foster says, "Freedom from anxiety is characterized by three inner attitudes. If what we have we receive as a gift, and if what we have is to be cared for by God, and if what we have is [to be made] available to others, then we will possess freedom from anxiety. *This is the inward reality of simplicity.*"[4]

> ... for I have learned to be content whatever the circumstances. I know what it is to be in need, and I know what it is to have plenty. I have learned the secret of being content in any and every situation, whether well fed or hungry, whether living in plenty or in want. I can do everything through him who gives me strength. (Philippians 4:11–13)

5. Reflect on those who seem to "have enough time."

> You are the light of the world. A city built on a hill cannot be hid. No one after lighting a lamp puts it under the bushel basket, but on the lampstand, and it gives light to all in the house. In the same way, let your light shine before others, so that they may see your good works and give glory to your Father in heaven. (Matthew 5:14–16, NRSV)

Your life choices matter to God. Along with your life gifts, spir-

---

[3]For a stimulating treatment of this topic, see Richard J. Foster, *Freedom of Simplicity* (San Francisco: Harper & Row, 1981).

[4]Richard Foster, *Celebration of Discipline*, revised edition (San Francisco: Harper & Row, 1988), p. 88.

itual gifts, and personality type, time is His gift to you. Good works are waiting for you—no one else can do them for you. But how do you find the time?

Think of people you greatly admire. Where do they get time to accomplish all they do? If you compare yourself to Jesus, whose ministry lasted only three years, you may feel overwhelmed before you begin. That's why the pages of *LifeKeys* are filled with more realistic models. Where did Marlys find the time to pack four hundred refugee boxes? Where did Jeff find the time to build a playground? And how did those church members sew all of those choir robes?

Guess what? You have the same amount of time available to accomplish whatever God chooses for you. For each of us the clock and calendar still tick off the same number of minutes in a day, days in a month, and months in a year. Yes, some of us sure seem to need more sleep and some of us will live longer, but from an eternal perspective we have more or less the same amount of time.

And each minute that you have comes from God. Are you a good steward of those minutes? Have you learned how to use your time so that someday you will hear, "Well done, good and faithful servant"?

It *is* possible. We have the promise that "he who began a good work in you will carry it on to completion until the day of Christ Jesus" (Philippians 1:6).

Work through the life choices exercises with an eternal perspective. Use your time with God this week to prayerfully examine your schedule, your priorities, and your lifestyle. Reflect on how God might ask you to change your life choices to find time for Him.

Prayer

Dear God,

It would be so much easier if You could be my appointment secretary, saying, "Yes" and "No" and "Not now, but later" for me. But I need to learn to live effectively in the here and now. Teach me how to make effective life choices. From here on, all my time is Yours. Teach me how to use it, setting aside time for You, time for others, and time to re-create myself, so that I can be ready to further serve You. Amen.

Thinking Through Your Life Choices

Listed below are four biblical principles for life choices we discussed:[5]

Your Ranking

1. Put first things first—seek the kingdom of God. _____
2. Know your mission. _____
3. Know your limits. _____
4. Simplify—aim for balance in your life. _____

- What does each of these principles mean to you? Write your own brief descriptions of each below.

- Then take a moment to rank the four principles in your own life, giving a (1) to the area you feel you manage the best and a (4) to the area where you believe you could most improve in making your life choices.
- Following each of the four biblical principles is a list of ideas recommended by our life choices experts—those who have taken our classes before—for gaining control of your life. For those principles you ranked (3) or (4), which ideas might help you? With your calendar in hand, consider what changes you might commit to in this season of your life as you work to create life choices which more truly reflect the person you are.

☐ *1. Put first things first—seek the kingdom of God.*

- Use commuting time for worship—with musical or devotional tapes.
- Buy a coffee maker with a timer—knowing that the coffee is waiting may help you get up a few minutes earlier for prayer.

---

[5]The fifth is discussed at length in the next chapter.

- Designate a special place in your home for worship—a chair, a closet, a room.
- Put time with God into your schedule before you plan anything else.
- Commit to a small group for worship or prayer.
- Keep track of the results in your life when you do not place God at the top of your list. Any motivators here?
- Schedule regular retreat times—perhaps even just an hour per week that you use as your time with God.
- If the method you choose isn't working, don't feel guilty. Try another suggestion!

What other suggestions might work for you?

☐ *2. Know your mission.*

- Give yourself several months if necessary to determine your mission (see Writing a Personal Mission Statement, page 241). Write out a mission statement and keep a visible reminder handy.
- Say no to things that keep you from your mission. Give yourself time to think by not saying yes too quickly.
- Don't set the bar so high that you are doomed to failure.
- As you work to discover your mission, pray that you will "know it." This may take months of thought.
- Schedule time seasonally for reflection and evaluation of your priorities in view of your mission and your changing life circumstances.

What other suggestions might work for you?

☐ *3. Know your limits.*

- Remember, even God rested on the seventh day!
- Let go of guilt. Take the *should*'s, *must*'s, and *have to*'s out of your vocabulary.

- Leave your date book at home so that you have time to consider each request and determine if it is in line with your personal mission.
- View saying no as allowing others the opportunity to develop or serve!
- Build time for self-care into your schedule.
- Use your mission to set priorities and parameters for your life and thereby know where to draw the line.
- Ask not only what you can do for others, but what they might be better off doing for themselves.

What other suggestions might work for you?

☐ *4. Simplify—aim for balance in your life.*

- Look at your activities, possessions, etc., as "overhead." Can you reduce or cut out anything and thereby be happier?
- Experiment with approaching an event, task, or celebration with simplicity, and discover the joy and freedom this may create.
- Don't give in to the clutter others say is necessary. Discern your own true needs.
- Establish your values so that you can more easily make decisions based on your own definition of simplicity.
- Stay away from stores and other distractions, unless you are shopping for or filling a specific need.
- Focus on what is *really* important for the day, perhaps the *one* most important activity.
- Focus on the eternal rather than on keeping up with the Joneses.

What other suggestions might work for you?

Review the four areas above. Are there ways you can adjust how you spend your time? Use this space to commit to one or two steps that will help you move your life choices toward the choices God would have you make.

My commitment:

  I will/will not

  1.

  2.

  By _____

LifeKey 8

Fulfillment is making music where God wants you to play.

CHAPTER 8

SERVICE—FOR WHOM WILL YOU PLAY?

We cling to a self-serving feeling of martyrdom about such a life of service. In actual fact, we are called to deny ourselves in order to open up to a more abundant life. In the exchange, the advantage clearly rests on our side: crusty selfishness peels away to reveal the love of God expressed through our own hands which, in turn, reshapes us into His image.[1]

—Dr. Paul Brand & Philip Yancey

A member of our congregation remarked, "I can easily summarize what it means to be a leader in the church. When I was promoted to the senior management team of my firm, I got a parking space with my name on it right by the door. When I became a church elder, I got to leave my car four blocks away to free up space in the church parking lot!"

Jesus made this point more than once: "... whoever wants to become great among you must be your servant, and whoever wants to be first must be slave of all" (Mark 10:43–44).

Servanthood is not a popular image in our society. The word evokes images of the disadvantaged, people at the beck and call of others, or menials with little time for their own needs. Often, this image of the woeful servant is layered onto Christian service until we believe, "If I am to serve, I shouldn't be happy, nor should I care for my own needs, because that isn't *holy*. I'll be a slave to others, belittling myself in the process—that's my fate if I want to be saintly."

Guess what? We are quite certain that this is *not* the biblical view of servanthood.

Biblical Servanthood

We read that as the Last Supper began, "Jesus knew that the Father had put all things under his power, and that he had come from God and was returning to God . . ." (John 13:3). So what did Jesus, with all the power of the world at His disposal, do next? Summon legions of angels? Perform great miracles that would sustain the faith of His disciples through the tumultuous events of the next few days? No, because He was confident in His own station, Jesus knelt and washed the disciples' feet.

True servants can perform *any* task—not because they think they are worth little or nothing but because they understand their own value in God's eyes. Jesus served from a place of power, not weakness. He stands ready to help you serve in the same way. How? To illustrate, let's look at Simon Peter.

We first meet Peter in a fishing boat, his nets empty despite a night of hard work. Jesus does not yet ask Peter to follow Him; He instead asks Peter to row out to deep water and again cast out the nets. Peter, with his fishing expertise, doesn't think much of this idea, but as he obeys, his nets, and the nets of James and John in the other boat, are so full of fish that they begin to break. "When Simon Peter saw this, he fell at Jesus' knees and said, 'Go away from me, Lord; I am a sinful man!' " (Luke 5:8).

This point at which Peter feels humiliated—when Peter feels worthless—is not when Jesus calls him to serve. Jesus first reassures this initial group of disciples that they need not be afraid. From now on they will do more than bring fish into a boat. They will work with Him to bring people into the Kingdom—they are worthy of this great commission. Jesus used the bulging nets of fish to show these early disciples not their own powerlessness but the power available to them through God as His servants.

> ### THE FIRST PRINCIPLE OF BIBLICAL SERVANTHOOD
>
> *Serve from a place of fullness, not emptiness.
> Jesus stands ready to fill your nets.*

If anyone had justification to serve from a place of shame or defeat, Peter certainly did. Even with the incredible advantage of being at Jesus' side for three years, Peter stumbled again and again until in the end he turned his back on the Lord. Read anew how on the night when Jesus was arrested, Peter denied being a disciple even as Jesus looked on:

> . . . another asserted, "Certainly this fellow was with him, for he is a Galilean."
>
> Peter replied, "Man, I don't know what you're talking about!" Just as he was speaking, the rooster crowed. The Lord turned and looked straight at Peter. . . . And [Peter] went outside and wept bitterly. (Luke 22:59–62)

Jesus did not ask the weeping Peter to found the Church, for He knew that a crushed and broken Peter couldn't communicate the life-changing message of the Resurrection. To ready Peter for his new role in the early Church, the Lord filled his nets once more.

After the Resurrection, the disciples returned to their fishing boats. Miserable in their failure to remain loyal to Jesus, they sought something familiar to them. Once again the disciples fished an entire night with nothing to show for their labor. A stranger on shore suggested they throw their nets on the other side of their boat. When they did, they caught so many fish that the nets were too heavy to pull into the boat. As John exclaimed, "It is the Lord," Peter was so excited that he jumped overboard with his clothes on!

Do you see how Jesus took Peter back to their beginning point, filling his nets with fish as a sign of His forgiveness? This Peter, now knowing forgiveness, could proclaim his joy even after being imprisoned and flogged for preaching about Jesus, "rejoicing because they had been counted worthy of suffering disgrace for the Name. Day after day, in the temple courts and from house to house, they never stopped teaching and proclaiming the good news that Jesus is the Christ" (Acts 5:41–42).

Servants who allow God to fill their cup are free to be used for God's purposes. They are secure, solid, and healthy enough to devote themselves to purposes bigger than themselves. They can confidently pursue their mission in life,

- using those instruments (life gifts and spiritual gifts) that God gave to them

- in places God has chosen for them (personality types)
- for God's agendas (values and passions).[2]

THE SECOND PRINCIPLE OF BIBLICAL SERVANTHOOD

Biblical servants ensure that their own needs are met so they can focus on the needs of others.

In the last chapter about life choices, we learned that God designed us to take time for ourselves, just as Jesus did. Jesus went to weddings, visited with friends, and took time for personal prayer. He made sure that He was full before pouring himself out to others.

Martin Luther wrote that when he was particularly busy, he found he could spend no less than *two* hours a day in prayer. Luther knew that his spiritual nourishment was crucial if he was to have the energy to serve others. Rest, recreation, and renewing your relationship with God are vital—God designed you to require them and in His eyes you *deserve* them. Joy-filled service happens when your own needs are satisfied in a way that lets you forget yourself so you can concentrate on the needs of others. Joy-filled service sometimes even feels like cheating because it is so full of satisfaction.

Servants who have learned to continually renew their own souls through the grace of God are then ready to take their eyes off of themselves and begin to search out where to use their gifts—those environments to which God calls them. Sometimes these service environments feel like a holiday. The environment is so enjoyable that it is as easy as a day at the beach. At other times, however, because God's purposes are often far-removed from the purposes of humankind, it may take some time and practice before joy surfaces.

The Gospel of Mark tells us that as Jesus prayed in the Garden of Gethsemane, He was deeply grieved, even to death (Mark 14:34). The cross was not the road to happiness or self-actualization, but it *was* the road to fulfillment.

There is a biblical difference between self-actualization and ful-

---

[2]Bolles, *What Color Is Your Parachute?*, p. 458.

fillment. As Jesus was being arrested, He said to the disciple who tried to defend Him, "Do you think that I cannot appeal to my Father, and he will at once send me more than twelve legions of angels? But how then would the scriptures be fulfilled, which say it must happen in this way?" (Matthew 26:53–54, NRSV). Think of the self-actualization Jesus would have experienced if, suddenly, the heavenly host had appeared to rescue Him. Picture what Hollywood could do with such a scene!

Yet Jesus chose *fulfillment.* His prayers before He was arrested make it clear that the choice *was* His—He had the same free will that you do to follow God's choices or your own choices. If you think Jesus' cosmic view of the consequences of His decisions gave Him a stronger will to do right than you could ever muster, then consider the disciples. The Gospels make it clear that these were *ordinary* men, just like you and me with our giftedness and our weaknesses. They *chose* to continue their mission despite dangers of persecution, shipwreck, imprisonment, and death. Yet they were able to claim, as did Paul: "Therefore I am content with weaknesses, insults, hardships, persecutions, and calamities for the sake of Christ; for whenever I am weak, then I am strong" (2 Corinthians 12:10, NRSV).

THE THIRD PRINCIPLE OF BIBLICAL SERVANTHOOD

Finding ways to use our giftedness for God requires conscious commitment. God leaves the choice of serving or not serving in our hands.

Choosing fulfillment over personal happiness was the key to Paul's commitment to serving God, just as it is for you today. If you grasp that you are making the choices God wants you to make—choices that will bring you and others fulfillment—you can more easily turn from using your gifts solely for your own personal and perhaps selfish happiness and turn toward using your gifts for God.

We choose our paths and our attitudes, but the more we let God influence our values and our passions the more we are available for His choices. Sometimes, though, you may not immediately feel that you are in the right spot. Many years ago a mother of three young children was once again at the endless job of cleaning the house. Feeling frustrated as she scrubbed the entryway floors, she complained, "God, I never have time for you anymore. My hours are filled being a nanny and housekeeper."

At that moment she felt the calming presence of God. She sensed His message to her. "But you are right where I want you, down on your knees where you can lift to me your prayers of praise and petition." The mother realized that one of God's missions for her life was a prayer ministry for others. Now that her children are grown, she continues daily worship and prayer for others. Down on her knees, working or praying or both, she has shown others the difference a love for Jesus can make—and she has found fulfillment for herself.

You may not immediately find contentment when you follow God's will. Like this young mother, you may be in the midst of your work before you realize what He has in mind. God doesn't promise happiness in each of the circumstances to which He calls us—but He does offer contentment to those who love Him enough to follow His leading.

Does this sound frightening—as if God leads us blindly toward horrendous hardships and battles? Well, what if you choose a different path? What if you choose circumstances other than what God has in mind for you? Corrie and Betsie ten Boom found God's calming answer to these questions. As they faced choices while the German armies overran their country, Betsie remarked, "The center of His will is our only safety—O Corrie, let us pray that we may always know it!"[3] As humans, we want to ask, "Couldn't we just...." or "Yeah, but...." Time and again, though, people who step in faith to the center of God's will eventually find that there is no place else they would rather be!

As A. W. Tozer put it, "Our insistence upon seeing ahead is natural enough, but it is a real hindrance to our spiritual progress. God has charged Himself with full responsibility for our eternal happiness and stands ready to take over the management of our lives the moment we turn in faith to Him."[4]

Is this the God in whom you have placed your faith? The One who is responsible for your eternity? The God who stands ready

---

[3]Corrie ten Boom, with John and Elisabeth Sherrill, *The Hiding Place*, p. 67. (Chosen Books, Inc., Chappaqua, New York. Used with permission).

[4]A. W. Tozer, *Knowledge of the Holy* (San Francisco: Harper & Row, 1961), p. 69.

to bring contentment to you in every circumstance—not happiness which could be superficial, but the deep-seated joy that comes through connecting yourself with the spirit of Christ?

THE FOURTH PRINCIPLE OF BIBLICAL SERVANTHOOD

As we open our hearts to God's purposes, we become available to move to the places where God wants us to be.

When Jesus heard of the illness of His dear friend Lazarus, He had choices to make. He could have healed Lazarus from a distance—He had done it before in healing the centurion's servant. He could have hurried to Bethany—His agenda was His own. He could have saved Mary and Martha a lot of worry by following their plan and healing their brother. However, He knew that was not what God had in mind. God's purpose in that hour was to demonstrate the power Jesus had over life and death, even His own death on the cross. Jesus knew this clearly: "For I have come down from heaven not to do my will but to do the will of him who sent me" (John 6:38).

Mary and Martha also believed themselves to be servants of God, but as they mourned the death of their brother, God's purposes escaped them. Both of them cried out to Jesus that if He had not tarried, Lazarus would not have died. They did not comprehend God's purposes until they heard the words of Jesus at the tomb and saw their brother living and breathing and walking once more.

Choosing to follow God's paths often results in these types of experiences—you believe you've done everything required of you, yet the situation worsens until you wonder if you really did choose correctly. The key to fulfillment is resting in the knowledge that you are within God's will rather than engaging in a futile search for worldly happiness.

THE FIFTH PRINCIPLE OF BIBLICAL SERVANTHOOD

Following God's leading does not always result in the world's approval. What will surely result is your own fulfillment as an instrument of God.

Paul says, "Am I now seeking human approval, or God's approval? Or am I trying to please people? If I were still pleasing people, I would not be a servant of Christ" (Galatians 1:10, NRSV). Paul's fulfillment came through knowing that he was carrying out purposes far greater than his own. When Paul was still Saul, he experienced self-actualization—he set his own goals and gained the respect of the religious authorities by persecuting the early Church. He tasted worldly success. Yet once he met God on the road to Damascus, he chose to find fulfillment by acting for God.

What Does a Modern Servant Look Like?

What are the first five things that come to your mind as you think of modern-day servants? Someone who is self-sacrificing, away from home, working with the poor? There are many, many people who are *en theos*, acting with God, in these ways, but these are not the only servants. Often, however, the Church celebrates this model of servanthood to the point that it is difficult to think of other types of servants. Compare your perceptions to the following people.

Consider what Dr. Allen, a professor of philosophy at Princeton Theological Seminary, once told his students: "Why was I chosen, out of hundreds of candidates, to chair this department? Sure, my Ph.D. is from Oxford and literally all of the top schools sought me for their staff, but why am I here? Because I was *called*. This is where God wants me for His purposes. Teaching is my calling, whether or not it perfectly fulfills my own interests—for if I could choose where to serve, it would be in a place like the Athens of ancient times, surrounded with other philosophers, filling my days with discourse and dialogue. But *here* is where God has called me, to influence my students."

Note that he didn't brag that he was the best philosophy professor available (although some would claim that he is!) but that he has been called to use his life gifts and spiritual gifts in this place, at God's calling—for what God has placed in his heart.

Listen, for a moment, to a successful businessman: "I don't know why God gave me a talent for making money, but I'm sure this is what I am meant to do. The more I make, the more I can give away. I can sponsor youth programs, send entire mission teams, donate to building efforts—if I left my work to serve the poor myself, I'd only be one set of hands. This way, I can multiply what I could do alone."

Note that his heart isn't ruled by making money, but by *giving* it away. He is a servant of God through and through, but in ways that are perhaps more hidden than the missionaries he supports, especially because he would rather give anonymously.

Or consider one family in India. David toured India as part of a missions/education group to survey the progress of various outreaches. The adults in one of the families David visited had attended seminary in the United States, then returned to their native country to serve. They chatted about life in America, and David mentioned some of the foods he craved and planned to eat as soon as he returned home. To David's astonishment, in a land where chickens and American-style bread were almost unheard of, he was served a plate of French toast the very next morning! David was left to wonder at the effort his hosts must have gone through to offer this luxury. The family had applied their ingenuity and their knowledge of David's homeland to serve him, a student, who had come to serve them.

THE SIXTH PRINCIPLE OF BIBLICAL SERVANTHOOD

The right place for you to serve is where God calls you to serve, whether far away or right where you are.

Biblical servants can be found everywhere today, from the board rooms of multinational corporations to the slums of overcrowded cities, from the laboratories of the great research hospitals to the streets where volunteers help children cross safely as they walk to school. Perhaps too many of us tend to confine servanthood to the exotic or unusual—and we know certainly that some of us are called to serve in such ways. But God also calls many of us to manifest a servant's heart *right where we are.* Often, He is simply waiting for us to lift our eyes to see what He is doing all around us!

How Do I Get From Here to There?

Maybe your journey isn't from here to there at all, but a series of small steps to realign who you are and what you do best. Service isn't necessarily *over there.* It may be *right beside you.* It may take time and effort to discover where God calls you to serve.

The answer, too, may be a process, not a single, life-changing call. Take a look back over your *LifeKeys*—your interests, your gifts, your personality, your passions, your values. What paths do they follow? You may not see the patterns until you come round the next bend.

For Jack, the pattern he saw in the end was amazing to him. Yet it was no surprise as he reviewed the values and passions that had influenced his life. For years his place to serve was right where he was. Primarily a businessman, Jack also knew that he valued God and wanted to help support those who chose missions work as their vocation. Growing up in a church where missionaries were the celebrated heroes, Jack knew firsthand many servants of God who went overseas. Family friends, home on furlough from the foreign countries, often dined with Jack's parents. As a boy, he loved to hear their stories. He saw his parents restrict their own spending to have more funds available to support several missions projects. Jack, however, never experienced "a call" to such work and went off to college to major in business.

Jack soon discovered his life gifts for negotiating, selling, and leading. By the age of thirty, he found himself an extremely successful businessman. His career led to settings that truly appealed to his personality. He loved the competitive atmosphere where he worked; information was the key ingredient to his trade, and he enjoyed every minute of the pursuit for the best tips and most current knowledge.

Success, however, did not turn Jack from his upbringing. He continually looked for ways to serve God other than the full-time missionary vocations that had been his childhood models. The "other ways," though, were hard for him to find. Jack and his wife sought causes to support out of their spiritual gift of giving—and soon found themselves contributing to several missions efforts. Jack also felt himself pulled toward planning teams at his church—especially planning for missions—acting through his spiritual gift of leadership. Serving together as a family at the Salvation Army on Christmas Day became a tradition. While he was thus able to be a servant as well as a businessman, Jack still felt disconnected from these tasks. The tasks did not present the interesting challenge that his profession did, nor were the atmospheres ones that really caught his attention.

As his fiftieth birthday drew near and as he reached the top of his profession, Jack realized one day that he was tired of competing: "It suddenly struck me that in order to be number one, I had to beat everyone else. I no longer wanted to see others lose. I wanted a different set of goals for my life, but I was afraid to leave the job that challenged me so completely. I needed that intellectual stimulation—that's how God made me."

While Jack was grateful for his success, he longed to do something significant—not necessarily in the eyes of the world, but something that would make a difference in the quality of life for other people. One afternoon, Jack ran into an old friend who had just completed an investigative visit to Uganda with an international organization that matched the skills of business leaders with the needs of people and projects in developing countries. As he heard his friend describe the educational, industrial, and financial consulting services these volunteer business people were providing to various organizations, Jack felt an inner excitement—missions work with a business twist! He had never been able to picture himself as a traditional missionary, but this program would put his business-oriented life gifts to work.

This "chance" encounter led to Jack's first visit to Africa, then to some training to develop skills that helped him fit into his new "mission" even more precisely, and finally to an early retirement so that he could serve in the places to which God was calling him. Besides a trip to Africa each year, he found new service projects that intrigued him all around his church and community—once he had the time and understood the ways God asked him to use his gifts. "I still use my hands to serve others, but I am confident that God wants me to use my money and my mind even more so.

"And when I travel under the auspices of a business endeavor, I can still do the work of God. Two years ago, because of my position as an 'expert,' I was able to convince a group of wealthy landowners that it made economic sense to pass on their knowledge of advanced agricultural techniques to their poverty-stricken tenant neighbors. When I returned to the area a few months ago, they had actually done it! Now their neighbors can produce enough food to feed themselves. The end of their vicious cycle of poverty may be in sight. The missionaries in the area hadn't been able to convince these farmers to love their neighbors, but in my role as a business leader, I was a part of breaking down that first barrier. Only a handful of people know that I played a role, but my joy in that role is far more significant than in any other business deal I ever made."

Your Path to Servanthood

God calls some of you to leave your boats and embark upon a whole new life as His servant. Some of you might stay in your current roles yet make other life choices that allow you to serve in new ways. Still others of you, like Jack, may find that the next season of your life brings together what God has been placing in your heart all along.

Whatever your own personal path, God has chosen it to fit your way of life, your giftedness, your own *LifeKeys*. Let God fill your nets as He shows you those good works already chosen for you.

Prayer

Dear God,

Help me to be a biblical servant, confident in how You have gifted me so that I can forget myself and become a part of Your purposes. Help me reach the point where it is more comfortable to know I am within the circle of Your will, no matter what that might mean, than anywhere outside Your will, no matter how safe that might seem. Show me the next steps. Amen.

CHAPTER 9

A FINAL NOTE OF ENCOURAGEMENT

There is nothing quite as exhilarating as getting out of bed in the morning, going back into the world, and knowing why. Enthusiasm is derived from the certainty that for this I was born, and I am doing it! It is thrilling knowledge that I am fulfilling God's intended purpose for me.[1]

—Bill Hull

Once upon a time in a faraway land lived a young girl named Nalia. In Nalia's country, each person's sixteenth birthday was celebrated with a great feast. At the end of the evening, the parents of the honoree announced the future of the child—the special gifts their son or daughter had and the way in which those gifts were to be used.

Being the youngest of four daughters, Nalia watched as each of her sisters heard the expectations for them. The oldest sister was

---

[1]Bill Hull, *Jesus Christ Disciple-Maker* (Colorado Springs: NavPress, 1984), p. 71.

a great musician, destined to beautify the lives of others through song. The next sister was a wonderful teacher who fostered a love of learning in her students. The third sister excelled in business, developing a recreational facility that provided rest and diversion to thousands of people each year.

As Nalia's sixteenth birthday drew near, she began to wonder what her future would hold. It seemed as if her sisters had every gift imaginable—what could possibly be left for her? "I'll probably end up with something I hate, stuck inside with too many people, instead of out in the gardens I love. Or worse yet, they'll assign me to something I can't do very well, like sales or singing with my sister."

As she pondered what she was sure would be a dismal future, she decided, "Why stay here at all? I'll run away before my party and make my own choices."

And that's just what Nalia did. Leaving her homeland behind, she went to work as a hired girl, spending most of her time cultivating the vegetable garden for the large household where she lived. Lonely, she often daydreamed about the beautiful flower gardens of the home where she had been raised and wondered how they looked. She had spent so many hours with their gardener, learning about the flowers and what made each one grow. "Well," she thought, "at least here I *am* outside, even if vegetables are rather dreary when compared to roses."

Years went by. One morning, as she cleared their breakfast table, she heard her mistress saying, "No, those aqua-tipped violets are no longer available. The gardener who used to care for them died several years ago and no one else in that land knew how to care for them."

Nalia wondered. *Her parents'* garden had been famous for its aqua-tipped violets. Could they be talking about her old friend the gardener? She just had to find out. Promising to return if she could, she packed her few belongings and caught a ride with a neighbor who happened to be traveling her direction.

Shy after being gone so long, Nalia approached her old home by the back way, not sure how she would be greeted if she went to the front door. To her horror, the beautiful garden was in ruins. What could have happened? Were all the members of her family dead? No, for she could hear her sister singing through the parlor window . . . and there was her mother, staring at her from the stable entrance.

"Nalia? It *is* you!" her mother cried as she ran toward her. As they hugged and assured each other that all was well, Nalia asked, "But what has happened to our flowers?"

With a sigh of sadness, her mother replied, "They were *yours*, for you to care for as soon as you turned sixteen. Only you had the passion and love of growing things to nurture this place when the old gardener retired. When you left, there was no one else to take your place. But now that you have returned, we can celebrate your feast, tell you of your path for the future . . . as soon as you tell us why you left."

What could Nalia say? That she had left because she assumed her parents—who had watched her, looking for her natural bent, the way she *should* go, her gifts, her passions, her values—would send her down a path of frustration? "I'm sorry . . . I didn't understand . . . but now I do and—let's celebrate!"

And, yes, they did live happily ever after, and the garden flourished as Nalia began the future for which she was designed. Your future can hold the same fulfillment as Nalia's, for yours is more than a fable. While our parents may not have the same insights as those in Nalia's country, God really does. And He has given us His word that we are here for a special purpose.

LifeKeys is an individual journey. Very few people complete such a journey in a few days, weeks, or even months; the progress varies greatly depending on where a person starts. As you finish these pages, you may be just at the beginning of your personal discovery. We encourage you to reread what you have learned about yourself several times over the next few weeks. This review process helps surface your *LifeKeys* in different ways until you understand what they mean for your future.

As we end each series of *LifeKeys* classes at our church, we hold a short prayer service. We return to the three underlying themes on which this book and this class are based, allowing people a chance to reflect on what these themes mean to them.

- *Do you believe that you are created in the image of God?* For many of our participants, the class has taken them further along the path. For the first time, they are able to say,

> "I am a valuable soul just as I am . . . even in the small things I do—God cares and loves me."

> "I now see myself as a person of value because God made me uniquely."

- *Do you believe that God has given you a special blend of life gifts, spiritual gifts, personality type, and values? That you are indeed fearfully and wonderfully made?* Some of our participants learn to celebrate their gifts, knowing that whatever they are, God chose those gifts specifically for them!

> "I'll never see my own abilities or those of others in quite the same way again!"

> "I'm no longer afraid to discover my gifts, for whatever they are, I know they are just right for me!"

- *Do you believe that God has planned good works for you to do?* A few of our participants find affirmation for areas of service or ministry that they have long contemplated. Others are ready to begin the search for the good works God has planned:

> "Now I am focused. I know my vision, my passions, and how to use my giftedness to ensure God's dream for me."

> "I think I am at the point, after a somewhat dormant season, to step out in faith and begin using gifts I've come to understand more clearly."

> "I commit to continue the process of discovering where my gifts can be used and having unwavering FAITH in the path I'm on, even as it changes and grows."

During a silent moment for personal reflection, we ask each person to offer up a commitment to God, placing their response to this question in an offering plate:

> As I leave this class, I want to make a commitment to action, be it in continuing on the journey of discovering what God has created me to be or in a new type of service for His kingdom:

The commitments range from promising to view themselves as

people of value to stepping out in faith to start new ministries.

What is your next step?

Can you say with your heart, in a paraphrase of Ephesians 2:10, "For I am fearfully and wonderfully made by God, created in Christ Jesus for good works, which God prepared in advance for me, to be my way of life"?

It is true—you are a valuable soul just as you are! Whatever God has chosen for your good works, they are chosen to fit your way of life, your calling, your mission. May these *LifeKeys* help you find true fulfillment.

LifeKeys Notations

I have identified the following life gifts (see page 48):

I have identified the following spiritual gifts (see pages 121–122):

With my personality preferences for ____ ____ ____ ____ (page 136) the following factors are important as I choose places or atmospheres:

My top eight values are (see page 175):

My passions (page 202), together with my other *LifeKeys*, indicate that I might act *en theos*, with God, in the following ways:

WRITING A PERSONAL MISSION STATEMENT

Imagine that it is 1492. You are standing on the deck of the Santa Maria. Adrift in uncharted waters, tossed and turned by forces in the sea and air, you are unsure of what direction to head yet desperate to stay on course. As night falls the stars appear one by one until they carpet the sky.

Finally you can roll out the maps, pull out your sexton, and hone in on the one thing that allows you to find your bearings. Yes, there's Ursa Major. You follow the pointer stars to Ursa Minor and the North Star. You jot down your measurements and set the ship's course.

Today, in the rapid waters of these times, a thoughtfully written mission statement is as important to us as the North Star was to Columbus. Your personal mission statement can act as your "North Star" as you make choices about the work you do and the purposes you will pursue. Especially for vocational choices in these changing times, your mission statement can help you view yourself as a "business"—outlining what you do best, where you prefer to operate, and for what causes or purposes you will act.

Don't be surprised if it takes you four or five tries—or four or five months!—to write a mission statement you consider adequate. Remember, you are creating a "North Star" for your life. As you read through the three sample mission statements given below, note how *different* they are.

My mission is to envision, communicate, and live out a model of a Christian man in America in the 1990s, in order to impact and empower as many people as I can over the longest period of time and to the deepest extent possible to further the kingdom of God.

241

I will do this by following the leading of the Holy Spirit and the following values I hope to model:

God and Jesus	beauty and natural things
healthy, balanced life	marriage
long-term friendships	love for learning
adventure and risk	organization
creativity and vigor	excellence
integrity and character	family
financial stewardship	self-respect
laughter	

My mission is to become, with God's guidance, the best Christian woman I can possibly be. I will do this by combining my life gifts of creativity and imagination together with my spiritual gifts of encouragement and leadership to effect positive changes in my life and in the lives of others.

I will give of myself and my time to my immediate world and to our larger world by volunteering, being there for others, and spreading the message of God's peace and love.

To be a creator and builder of things that enrich others' lives and bring beauty and harmony into the world.

To uplift, to celebrate, and to help grow everyone I can through word and deed, so that they may better know their own worth and, through me, know the unconditional love of God.

As a husband, to continually build an ever-growing, nurturing synergistic relationship.

As a father, to always love, nurture, and encourage our children to become growing and contributing human beings who, in achieving their potential, love themselves, God, others, and nature.

As an executive, to create working environments where all feel they are growing and contributing. To lead my company based upon high principles, thereby affirming those principles to stockholders and contributing to society.

As a part of the family of man, I am an employee of God; in His business of transforming lives.

Now review your responses in LifeKeys Notations, as you work your way through the following four steps:

1. Write one or two sentences that describe your *life gifts* and *spiritual gifts*, in order to summarize the things you do well.

2. Reread your observations about your personality type (pages 130–137) and your passions summary, page 202. Write one or two sentences that describe the atmosphere where you would most likely choose to use your life gifts and spiritual gifts.

3. From your *values* summary (page 175), adding from *passions* if appropriate, write out the purposes that really matter to you, the ones you would likely act upon.

4. Bring your three sets of sentences together into one paragraph.

Discover the Keys to Life...

LifeKeys is a revolutionary new approach to self-discovery—determining all you were created to be so you can live effectively for God. Most personality "tests" or spiritual gift inventories look at only one or two elements of who you are. *LifeKeys* looks at five elements, including your personality, values, talents, passions, and spiritual gifts. Ideal for group or individual use.

LifeKeys
—Jane A.G. Kise, David Stark, Sandra Krebs Hirsh *$14.99*

• Helps you choose a career, ministry, talent, and pastimes that offer satisfaction and maximize your potential.

• **Workbook** (*$6.99*) offers the excercises of *LifeKeys* in an easy-to-use, economical format.

"LifeKeys makes it practically impossible not to come away with a profound sense that God created you uniquely, values you highly, and has good works in mind for you. I recommend LifeKeys for anyone seeking to integrate faith and life."
—Janet O. Hagberg, Author of *The Critical Journey*

Find Your Fit: LifeKeys for Teens
—Jane A.G. Kise and Kevin Johnson *$10.99*

• Provides youth leaders, counselors, parents, and Christian schools with a resource to help guide their teens through tumultuous times.

• Features exercises, quizzes, spiritual gifts inventories and more created specifically for older teens grappling with difficult questions of identity and God's place for them in the world.

• **Workbook** (*$6.99*) Presents the talent, interest, and personality discovery exercises of the *Find Your Fit* in an engaging manner.

"We wish we'd had this book when we were 17!"
—Sigmund Brouwer & Cindy Morgan, bestselling author and Dove Award-winning recording artist

HELP FOR *LifeKeys* LEADERS

LifeKeys is an organized approach for people to discover who they are, why God made them, and what they do best—orchestrating all the ways God has gifted them. However, the expectations and takeaway of readers and participants in our *LifeKeys* seminars often vary widely. When we polled one class, we received the following list of expectations:

- Improved self-awareness—increased ability to recognize sources of stress and to discern healthy and unhealthy emotions
- Better husband-wife communications
- Learning to appreciate the gifts I have, mourn those I do not have
- Develop a framework for all that is "rumbling around" inside of me
- Stop being mismatched with church and other jobs
- Develop better ties between my vocational gifts and my spiritual gifts

- Decide what I want to be "when I grow up"—in the next season of my life
- To be recharged spiritually
- Discern the difference between what I want to be and what God wants me to be
- To kindle joy
- To overcome a fear of using a gift—or having to step out in unknown territory
- To discover new gifts

Because *LifeKeys* enables people to discover themselves with new, deeper meaning, it brings to the surface many issues and is used by God in many different ways. Consequently, it is important for you to create a caring atmosphere when you lead participants through this material. Prepare small group leaders to help people with the process and establish prayer support because some people will explore the very core of their being.

As a practical help to you we have provided these guidelines to give you a structure for using these materials. Our suggestions fit an eight-week class or small-group experience, though you can easily modify our suggestions to fit other formats.

Format Options

Eight-Week Course

In our experience, an eight-week course is the most successful format. The eight-week time frame allows time for processing the many discoveries people make about themselves along the way. Each session needs to be at least ninety minutes long to allow time for topic introduction, small group interaction, and questions.

The first classes at our church were shorter—and we ended up holding midweek help sessions to answer individual questions. Over half the class attended the help sessions, which led us to expand our class time to at least ninety minutes.

Two-Day Seminar

This course can be taught in a retreat setting or as a two-day seminar. If you decide to use this option, we recommend assigning some of the materials in advance of attendance. This allows more time for participants to ask questions and spend time in small group discussions, and to tie together what each person has learned. Advance work could include reading over the sections on life gifts (pages 38–48) and personality types (pages 138–153). It may also be helpful for them to preread the entire chapters on passions and life choices to give time for the concepts introduced in those chapters to begin to take root.

By now you have realized that we are suggesting participants preread almost all of the materials! This is because so much of LifeKeys is *processed over a period of time*. It might be better to focus the retreat on one or two topics that benefit the most from lecture and small group exercises, such as life gifts, spiritual gifts, and personalities. You could then address the topics of life choices and service during chapel times or evening inspirational talks.

Using LifeKeys in Established Small Groups

Ongoing groups of all shapes and sizes can follow our design for the eight-week format. Assign both reading and exercise completion before the small group meeting time.

Highlighting Individual Modules

Each of the discovery modules (life gifts, spiritual gifts, personality types, values, and passions) can be used by itself for more intensive study. The chapters are designed to be stand-alone pieces and have been used for training, team building, adult education classes, marriage enrichment, and other areas. We suggest concentrating on one unit at a time, with the following recommendations for these uses:

- *New member assimilation:* We suggest using *life gifts* to help newcomers match their gifts with volunteer opportunities. Studies suggest that not all new members are ready for the deeper topic of spiritual gifts.
- *Leadership development:* We suggest using *spiritual gifts*, encouraging leaders to envision ministries that align with the gifts they have.
- *Marriage enrichment:* We suggest using *personality types* and

values to foster communication and understanding by gaining insights into how others function and the values they choose to live.

- *Team building:* We suggest using *life gifts* and *personality types* to understand how each team member will function best. The *passions* chapter can lend insights as to the motivations and expectations of those who will be working together.

Before You Begin—Team Formation

If you plan to offer *LifeKeys* in its entirety in a class setting, we recommend forming a team to handle class preparation and implementation. A sample schedule for team formation is as follows:

Three months in advance

1. Pull together a team interested in using gift indentification to empower people. Team size may vary from two to eight individuals, depending on the members' interests, time availability, and life gifts. The following roles may be needed:

   - Team leader
   - Publicity manager: Publicize the course, answer questions.
   - Teachers: Seek people from your congregation or organization who might have experience in vocational counseling or human resources development, MBTI® practitioners, and others who may have completed a process similar to *LifeKeys*. (See 3 and 4, next page.)
   - Registration and administration manager: Coordinate registration, possibly handle classroom arrangements and setup.
   - Small group coordinator: Train small group leaders and instruct them for each class time.[1] (We highly recommend that each member of the project team also serve as a small group leader for the course.)
   - Volunteer liaison: Compile a list of various volunteer or service opportunities available in the church or organization for participants who are ready to act on what they have learned about themselves.

---

[1]We recommend a minimum of one to two hours of basic training on how to lead small groups, using a curriculum such as *People Together*, by David Stark and Patrick Kiefert, available through Church Innovations: (612) 646–7633.

2. Set dates and locations for the class to be held. Order *LifeKeys* and other supplies and reserve any needed audio-visual equipment.

3. Review the curriculum. Ideally, the team will journey together through *LifeKeys*, scheduling sessions to cover each unit. Knowing the book's content and intent as well as each person's own gifts and experiences with each *LifeKey* will allow the team to be of maximum help to others. And doing these exercises together can help with team-building.

4. Decide who will teach which units. The *LifeKeys* of life gifts, spiritual gifts, and personality types may require more background reading and preparation.

5. Life gifts are based on the same theory as the Strong Interest Inventory™[SII], but we do not offer the Strong as part of our classes. The person assigned to teach this unit may want to check the suggested reading list (page 271) for background resources. If you have a person who is qualified to give the SII, you may want to offer this additional service to participants.

We *do*, however, routinely allow people to take the MBTI,® although it is not necessary to do so. While the materials contained in Chapter 4 are sufficient to introduce the applications of type for discovering the places or atmospheres that have the most appeal to them, many of our participants appreciate the opportunity to take the actual inventory. Because the MBTI® is so widely used, check with members of your congregation to see if anyone is a qualified user. If not, you can prepare an excellent presentation with extra study of *LifeTypes*, by Sandra Krebs Hirsh and Jean Kummerow, or *Work It Out*, by Sandra Krebs Hirsh with Jane Kise. (See suggested reading.)

6. Begin to work with the congregation's or organization's staff on how class participants can connect with service opportunities after completing *LifeKeys*. Some organizations have systems in place for matching people with positions. For other organizations, you will need to initiate this process. It may be sufficient to identify ministries and the types of work involved in those ministries, enabling people to review "job descriptions."

If you are using *LifeKeys* within a church, identify both positions within the church as well as those with outreach or parachurch ministries that the church supports or works with regularly.

It is our experience that while not all participants are ready to make service commitments at the end of the course (and some are already extensively involved in volunteer work), most want to understand how their own church could aid them in finding the volunteer opportunities that fit them best.

Setup for Class Meeting Time

From the first meeting, we suggest that participants be assigned to a small group of six to eight people and that the small groups be seated at round tables if possible. The small groups help establish a sense of community and an avenue for seeking help.

Note: As you graduate a class of *LifeKeys* participants, ask for volunteers to be small group leaders for subsequent sessions. These volunteers receive the added benefit of taking the class again and usually gain new or extra insights from a second or even third exposure to the materials. *We* have learned so much each time we've taught the class. Also, watch for potential project team leaders and potential teachers to expand the opportunities for more people to take the class.

- Have premade name tags available (first names in large print to ensure readability) that can be reused each week. Put the person's group number on the back of the tag so they can easily find their group each time. Collect the name tags at the end of each session.
- Place group numbers on the tables. Small group leaders should try to be the first to arrive to make it easier for others to find their spots.

Session 1: Introduction to *LifeKeys*

During the first session we want to make sure we establish:

An atmosphere of affirmation. With each exercise, we want people to feel good about themselves and about what they discover. Because participants are dealing with self-identity, issues of self-esteem do surface throughout the course. Many of the objectives and exercises we recommend for this first session are aimed at creating the right atmosphere so that participants like what they learn about themselves.

A sense of community. Have people enrolled in the class think about it as being on an adventure together where everyone learns from each other.

A process which focuses on people. The small groups play a crucial role in keeping the focus on the needs of the participants rather than on the intricacies of various inventories.

Classtime Flow

1. **Welcome** (30 minutes)

   Distribution of materials, introduction of leadership team.

   General instructions:

   - The schedule and class exercises assume participants have preread the assigned chapters and have completed the exercises in advance.

   - Instruct participants to set aside 1–3 hours per week to read the materials and complete the exercises in order to benefit fully from the next class session.

   - Some of the exercises—especially the ones on *passions*—cannot be rushed. Participants may even need several weeks to reflect on their answers.

   - Clarify how participants can learn of assignments or get help if they miss a class. For our classes, participants may contact their small group leaders for assignments and questions, etc.

   - Participants may need help as they work through these very important aspects of their lives. Clarify how individual help beyond class time can be sought.

   Class "rules of operation":

   - Things shared within the small groups are to be kept *confidential.*

   - There are no *right* or *wrong answers* for much of this material.

   - There is no such thing as a stupid question.

- We will start and end on time.

- We will try to give equal "air time" to each participant. The small group leaders will facilitate to make sure this happens.

2. **Class expectations** (10 minutes)

Ask the entire group for expectations they have for the class, or discuss expectations in table groups. After 5–10 minutes, ask each table group to name one of their expectations; move on to the next table group; continue the process several more times until all expectations have surfaced. Record the expectations on a flip chart or blackboard so that everyone can see them. *Be sure to copy and keep them so the project team can refer to them throughout the course for refining class time and to remind participants at the conclusion of the class what was on their minds and hearts when they started.*

3. **Small group time—getting acquainted** (20 minutes)

Objective: Getting acquainted. Most participants do not come ready to share at a deep level, so our questions start with ones that people can share at a level they find comfortable. List (at most) three of the following questions, allowing each participant to choose the one they prefer to discuss:

- Tell us the history behind any part of your name—first, middle, or last. How did your parents choose your name?

- Did you have a favorite nickname growing up? How did you come to get that name?

- Some people would rather rename themselves if they had a chance. What name would you give yourself?

- As a child, was there something you wanted to be when you grew up? What was that? Have you stuck to that dream? If not, what made you change your mind?

- Share one of your favorite experiences. This experience could be work related, a committee or task force on which you participated, a school activity, a social club, a hobby that you enjoy, a vacation or social gathering you helped plan, or a service or volunteer experience. What made it so enjoyable?

4. **Introductory lecture** (30 minutes)

Refer to Chapter 1 to formulate your lecture. Main objectives for the lecture:

- This class is the beginning of a process. Most people will continue to work on what they have learned long after the last session.

- Participants will vary in how they approach *LifeKeys*. Some people will breeze through the exercises, some will want to savor each one, and others will need time and encouragement to get through. Still others may wish to use outside resources available to them.

- There are no ungifted people! The Bible promises us that. If anyone struggles with discovering how they are gifted, ask them to come to the leadership team for help.

- God has created us, according to His plan, for a purpose. This class begins the process of discovering what He would have each of us do, the places or environments where we can best use our gifts, and the causes or situations for which we would most like to put them to use.

Be sure to allow time for general questions about the class.

Session 2: Life Gifts

We chose to begin with life gifts because they fit well within the Richard N. Bolles mission paradigm (page 29). Everyone can successfully identify at least one interest pattern. Life gifts also fall in neutral territory (in contrast with spiritual gifts) for participants who are struggling with the idea of whether they are indeed created with gifts from God.

Classtime Flow

1. **Introductory Lecture** (20 minutes)

Refer to Chapter 2 to plan your lecture. Key objectives:

- To explain the concept of life gifts and to make the point that every individual has special interest patterns.

- To introduce the life gifts exercises. Allow time for questions, and provide participants with sufficient directions to complete the exercises on their own.

2. **Large Group Exercise** (20 minutes)

A fun way to introduce the six interest themes is by having the participants self-select their top interest theme as they hear each theme described.

- In advance assign one of your small group leaders to each of the six interest areas. Make signs for each of the interest areas and post them in the room (or give one to each small group leader to hold), following the hexagon order (Realistic—Investigative—Artistic—Social—Enterprising—Conventional).

- Inform the group that they will be constructing a "living hexagon." Have everyone gather around the Realistic sign as you describe that area, using pages 39–40 of *LifeKeys*.[2] People who feel this description describes them can stay at that sign; others move on as you describe the Investigative gift, and so on, around the hexagon of interest areas. Tell the participants that they can move to another interest area later if they feel that it describes them better.

- If you are doing *LifeKeys* in a church setting, as you discuss each interest area, ask what people with these interest patterns might enjoy as volunteer opportunities:

Realistic—maintenance, out-of-doors experiences, transportation, building or other hands-on service

Investigative—research, apologetics, computer systems design, long-range planning

Artistic—music, one-time creative efforts, bulletin design, drama teams, decorating

Social—teaching, counseling, organizing social gatherings,

---

[2]For extra special help, purchase *Strong Interest Inventory Resource: Strategies for Group and Individual Interpretations in Business and Organizational Settings*, by Sandra Krebs Hirsh, available from Consulting Psychologists Press (800–624–1765). While written for the Strong Interest Inventory,® it has many reproducible masters and exercises to enrich your presentation of the material on life gifts.

small group leadership, hospitality

Enterprising—leadership, building campaigns, member involvement, new ministry development, evangelistic efforts

Conventional—office tasks, finance, standing committees, record-keeping, establishing procedures, ushering

- When you have finished describing each of the six themes, people will be grouped in the areas that are of most interest to them. Have them sit down in these groups to discuss the life gifts found in their particular interest area.

3. **Small Group Exercise** (30 minutes)

Within the interest area groups formed above, have each group discuss and prepare to report on the following:

- What elements of the description of the interest area best fit each participant?
- What would we like the other groups to know about us? Have each group develop a list to report to the other groups.
- Which of the life gifts have the participants used?

4. **Closing** (20 minutes)
   - Have each of the interest area groups report on what they'd like the others to know.
   - Explain the life gifts exercise pages, using directions on pages 48–49. Ask people to come to the next class with their possible life gifts highlighted on their summary hexagon of interest areas (pages 52–53).
   - Allow time for questions.

5. **Optional small group exercise to affirm life gifts** (15 minutes. This could be used in a help session or to open a later class.)

Ask groups to discuss one of the following:

- The church's fiftieth anniversary (or a community event) is coming up and a huge celebration is planned. With which part of the celebration (decorations, program planning, refreshments, publicity, finances, child care, entertainment, cleanup, etc.) would you like to help? Which life gifts would you be using?

- Which people in the group have similar life gifts? What are the settings or places where you use those gifts, and how diverse are those settings?

- Which is one of your favorite life gifts? When did you first become aware that this was one of your gifts? How have you developed it? How are you currently using it?

- Let each participant discuss the life gift they most enjoy using. Have them try to describe it in one sentence and then give an example of when they have put that life gift to use.

- List six volunteer opportunities available in your church or organization during the next three months. Identify the kinds of life gifts that might be needed for each opportunity.

Session 3: Introduction to Spiritual Gifts

Participants vary widely on how much exposure they have had to spiritual gifts. Our approach to spiritual gifts is meant to help "beginners"—those who have never had sufficient exposure to spiritual gifts to feel comfortable with the concept and ready to identify possible places of giftedness. George Barna's survey says that only 31% of adults who have *heard* of spiritual gifts are able to *identify* even one that they possess.[3] In contexts that emphasize spiritual gifts our approach may seem basic, but research shows that the majority of Christians lack depth of knowledge in this area.[4]

1. **Introductory lecture on spiritual gifts** (20 minutes)

   Refer to Chapter 3 to prepare your lecture. Key teachings:

   - To understand what spiritual gifts are and how they differ from life gifts. Unlike life gifts, spiritual gifts are given to further God's purposes.

   - To have participants know that spiritual gifts are not given

---

[3]Barna, p. 1.
[4]For more on this research, request the October 3, 1995, press release from Barna Research Group, Ltd., entitled, "Most Christians Are Oblivious to Their Spiritual Gifts," (818) 241–9300.

based on our merit but graciously given to meet the needs of the Church. There are no "superior" gifts.

2. **Lecture on specific gifts** (50 minutes)

We find it beneficial to "teach through" each of the gifts, allowing for individual questions and, after a gift has been explained, asking for a *show of hands* from participants who believe they possess each gift.

We also *consistently* find ourselves short of time for this lecture, because of participants' great interest in the subject. While the entire next week is devoted to personality types, it is possible to shorten the exercises in week five (Values) to allow more time for spiritual gifts. By that point, people will have also read through the descriptions and probably identified their gifts. This is a good time to come back and answer further questions.

Hint: you will want to be ready to address the differing theologies concerning the sensational gifts such as speaking in tongues and healing. Many people have questions about them. Make sure that you are clear on the potential overlap among the gifts of knowledge, prophecy, discernment, and wisdom.

3. **Optional small group exercise** (15 minutes)

Have participants read the following scenario on their own and respond to the first question *by themselves*.

Leah and Rob Hunter are members of a local church. They have two daughters, ages five and two, and are expecting their third child in three months. Rob's job requires sporadic travel. In addition, Rob has sole responsibility for the care of his elderly grandmother, now in a nursing home. Leah had just been informed that to prevent early delivery, she must be hospitalized for the next four to eight weeks, with total bed rest and intravenous drugs prescribed. The drugs they will give her to prevent the premature birth of the child could damage her own internal organs and might not successfully prevent early delivery. A previous pregnancy ended in a stillborn child, and she is extremely anxious over the health of this baby.

If the baby is delivered successfully, Leah has been told

to expect a lengthy recovery time for herself and the newborn.

a. List a few of the needs this family would have. Then individually choose the one you would be most interested in responding to and describe what you would do to help.

b. Share your responses as a group. How do the various responses reflect your differing spiritual gifts? Your life gifts?

c. It is also helpful to come back together as a large group and put all of the responses on a board. The leader can then summarize the diverse ways in which people with different spiritual gifts would help. The Body of Christ needs *all* the gifts!

Session 4—Personality Types

Within the framework for *LifeKeys*, we now turn from the question of what we *do* (life gifts and spiritual gifts) to understanding the types of *atmospheres* where we might choose to do those things.

Personality type does not explain everything about people. It does, however, do an excellent job of helping them understand themselves, appreciate others, know the work/volunteer setting best for them, and make sense of some of their life choices.[5] Personality type can be used for many other purposes, but with the time available it will be important to stick to using type *to guide participants to the places that are the most appealing to them.*

Note: We administer the MBTI® before this class session, using the last few minutes of the previous class to give instructions. While the chapter on personality type allows people to select an approximate type, many find the MBTI® a helpful check of what they selected. Many people are qualified to administer the MBTI.® If no one on your staff is qualified, check with other members of your congregation. You may also call the Association for Psychological Type (816–444–3500) to find qualified people in your area.

---

[5]For a fuller treatment of psychological types, you can read and/or refer others to *LifeTypes*, by Sandra Krebs Hirsh and Jean Kummerow, and *Work It Out*, by Sandra Krebs Hirsh with Jane A. G. Kise (see suggested reading list).

Classtime Flow

1. **Lecture on preferences** (30 minutes)

   Refer to Chapter 4 to prepare for your lecture. Key points:

   - Everyone has a distinct personality type—most likely determined before our birth but subject to modification by environmental influences.

   - Understanding type gives insights into people and the work settings and styles with which they are most comfortable, as well as insights into their relationships.

   - Personality types are God-given. There are no "good" or "bad" types. Each has a unique contribution to make.

   - Discuss each of the eight preferences, allowing people to self-select the preferences that seem to fit best.

   - Discuss how preferences influence the settings in which we choose to work.

2. **Large group exercise** (30 minutes)

   Divide the room by placing a piece of masking tape across the floor. Designate the front of the room as the "top" and the back of the room as the "bottom" of the Human Type Table. Have those with a preference for Introversion move to the front of the room and those with a preference for Extraversion move to the back. Then divide the room again, this time with "left" and "right" sides to represent the left and right sides of the type table. Ask everyone to stay where they are in regard to the top and bottom of the room, but have those with a preference for Intuition move to the right side of the room. This now creates four quadrants. While you will want to add your own comments to the description of each quadrant (see Suggestions for Further Reading, page 271) you might mention the following:

   - Those in the IS (top left) quadrant enjoy settings that honor past experience: "What has worked for us before?"

   - Those in the EN (bottom left) quadrant enjoy settings that honor change and innovation: "We've already done it that way; let's try something different this time."

- Those in the IN (top right) quadrant enjoy settings where they can develop and promote the ideas that call for change.

- Those in the ES (bottom right) quadrant enjoy settings that are action-oriented, seeking to change or improve on something: "Let's just do it."

(Note: Opposite quadrants are described sequentially to make the contrasts more vivid.)

With the masking tape, divide the room into four "columns," with two on the right and two on the left side of the room. Then have those with a preference for Thinking move to the outer left or right columns; those with a preference for Feeling are to move to the inner columns.

- Those in the ST column concentrate on the present and on the specific facts: "What do the facts tell me about how to fix the problem in the most practical way?"

- Those in the SF column also concentrate on the present and specific facts: "How can I use this information to help the people around me feel better today?"

- Those in the NF column concentrate on the future and the big picture: "How can I use this information to help people realize their potential?"

- Those in the NT column also concentrate on the future and the big picture: "How does this help me understand the system, its structure, or grasp a universal truth?"

Divide each of the top and bottom portions of the room into two rows each with the masking tape. Have those with a preference for Judging move to the very bottom and the very top rows, where they can help "keep order." Have those with a preference for Perceiving stay in the middle two rows. This last division of the type table forms type-alike groups.

3. **Small group exercise** (15 minutes)

Have people sit with their "type-alike" group. If there are types with a sole representative, ask that individual to be a group of one so that he or she can report to the rest of the group about the characteristics of that type. Using pages 138–153, the type descriptions, allow them to discuss what insights their types give them in choosing environments or settings.

If there is time, let each group briefly report to the large group three things that they would most like the other types to know about them.

Caution: Class time is very short. Most MBTI® practitioners prefer three hours to introduce the concepts. If you administer the MBTI,® you may want to schedule additional time for this session.

Session 5: Values

The subject of values helps many participants turn from focusing on how God has gifted them to how they might use their gifts for God's purposes. Not all will be ready to make that turn; some will still be preoccupied with trying to accept and validate what they have learned so far about themselves.

Classtime Flow

1. **Introduction and card sort instructions** (10 minutes)

   Use Chapter 5 to prepare for the introduction. Key points:

   • Everyone has a set of values that affects how he or she spends time and uses energy and resources.

   • Christians can legitimately hold different values. Some things in the Bible are black and white, but many are disputable. (Romans 14:1 is a good reference.)

2. **Values card sort** (30 minutes)

   Give the participants room to spread out their values cards found at the back of *LifeKeys*. Using the instructions on page 174, explain how to set up their prompt cards. Establish the frame of mind with which they should approach the card sort.

   Warn them in advance that it may be hard to limit their top values to eight—but gently force them to do so.

   When they have completed their sort, have them record their

values on the Values Summary Sheet (page 175).

Hint: We find that people enjoy sorting their cards while interacting with the members of their small group. People approach the task in a variety of ways and the group atmosphere adds encouragement to what can be a difficult task for some.

3. **Small group exercise** (15 minutes)

Discuss question 4, page 178, of the values exercise:

Assume that you have found a job or service opportunity that fits with your life gifts, spiritual gifts, and personality type. What is the atmosphere needed for it to match with your top eight values?

4. **Lecture on values** (30 minutes)
   - Being aware of their values helps people understand their priorities, clarify their choices, and discern what will give meaning to their lives.
   - God wants to influence values. Values are not given by God in the way He gives spiritual gifts and personality type.
   - Awareness of their top eight to ten values helps people work through conflicts and understand the nature of the situations that trouble them the most. Values become most evident in conflict situations.
   - People's values can change over their lifetime due to circumstances.
   - Allow time for questions. Emphasize that participants should choose just a few questions in the values exercises (pages 176–181). The values questions are suggested for different circumstances such as:
     —facing the next season of life
     —selecting work/service environments
     —evaluating lifestyle choices
   - (Optional) Discuss drafting a personal mission statement. Suggestions for doing so are given on pages 241–243. Con-

sider scheduling a help session for those who are interested in pursuing this.

Session 6: Passions

We now move to specifically identify those good works God prepared in advance for each individual (Ephesians 2:10). For many, this can be the most frustrating part of the course. Our society traps so many people in the bustle of day-to-day pressures that to dream about possibilities and future actions aimed at helping others or improving society seems burdensome rather than a route to fulfillment.

The passions introduction seeks to give positive examples of people whose passions arose out of their current activities or who were easily able to find a channel through which they could act on their passions. This approach helps participants to be open-minded to finding out what God has put in their hearts, be it large or small in scope.

Classtime Flow

1. **Introduction** (30 minutes)

   Ask two or three members of your congregation or organization to explain one of their passions to the class. Interview them regarding how they live out a passion or dream—what it is, how it developed, and what they see as their next steps. Make sure that small as well as large passions are described, ranging in scope from collecting toys for the church nursery to a citywide food drive, for example.

   As an alternative, we sometimes use an outside resource for this introduction. *Wrestling With Angels,* a six-part video series from Zondervan Publishing House, has a wonderful interview with Tony Campolo, noted Christian author, on the subject of knowing God's will.

   Refer to Chapter 6 to prepare your lecture. Key points:

   - Passions can be described as a strong devotion to a task, an excitement about something, or a willingness to stand up for a cause or belief.

- Sometimes God places passions in our hearts for His purposes. These passions may be wide or narrow in scope and long-term or short-term in commitment.

- Passions readily shift and change over the course of a lifetime.

- Passions surface in many ways—out of our gifts, out of people we encounter, or out of life events. We find (and our exercises are built around that experience) that people sort into four different approaches in finding their passions:

The "Dreamers"—those who can easily think of places to act *en theos,* with God. Joseph might be a biblical example.

The "One Talent" people—those who are passionate about using a single life gift or spiritual gift in many arenas. The craftsmen who built the tabernacle in Exodus 30–31 might be an example.

The "Make Me an Offer" people—those who are willing to help people with their passions if they just knew the need. Stephen and the other deacons of the early Church in Acts 6 might be an example.

The "Right Under Your Nose" people—those who can serve right where they are. Dorcas, in Acts 9, might be an example.

2. **Small group time** (20 minutes)

Have each participant talk about a possible passion they have identified. Have they been chewing on this possibility for a long time or is it a new thought? Can they begin to act now or is this passion for the future? What do they need to do now to get ready to act on this passion? How does this passion mesh with what they have discovered about their gifts and talents?

If some people seem stuck or uncertain of specific causes, people, or places that might energize them, have them look at their life gifts or spiritual gifts for information on what they might like to do.

Hint: Some participants may not think that their passions are "big enough." Small group leaders may need to assume a teaching role on how God sees both big and small needs in the world, each just as important as the others.

Others may not have surfaced any passions. Sometimes the group can see patterns for passions if a person is willing to share their life gifts, spiritual gifts, and values. One recent retiree said that she didn't seem passionate about anything but baking bread, her current hobby. Her small group encouraged her with ways she could share her home-baked bread with others—for communion, with shut-ins, etc. The woman was encouraged that doing little things, not necessarily devising a grandiose plan, may be just what God intended for her.

3. **Lecture—How God Makes Dreams Happen** (30 minutes)

Consider using the story of Joseph (see *Living With Your Dreams* in Suggestions for Further Reading) as background for this lecture. Nehemiah (see page 184) is also a good example. Key points:

- Dreams often need tempering and developing.

- Dreams often change over time.

- The *dreamer* may often need to be refined.

- It is seldom a straight line from where you are to your dream—your course may meander.

- Sometimes dreams are shattered, but God has the power to reshape them into something else.

- At times it seems that a dream or passion could never come true, but it may be important to stay open and remember that life has many seasons and the time may not yet have come.

Session 7: Life Choices

There are *many* time-management tools available. Our purpose is to highlight some of the biblical concepts of time and the choices we make. This session often legitimizes the doubts people have about the next steps they might take and lets them discuss their concerns with others who struggle with similar issues. The topic of life choices also puts into perspective how God might help people take those next steps.

Classtime Flow

1. **Opening exercise** (10 minutes—as people gather)

   Have participants answer one of the following questions:

   • As you look back through your list of top values, what activities are missing from your current life that would have a tremendous impact on your ability to live out these values?

   Hint: This could be used as a small group discussion question if time allows and the groups have grown close.

   • Think over your activities during the past week and figure out what percentage of your time went to the following activities:

      time for work

      time for self

      time for God

      time for leisure activities

      time for family

2. **Lecture** (30 minutes)

   Refer to Chapter 7 to prepare your lecture. Also, refer to the suggested reading list (page 271) for other background materials. Key points:

   • Start by emphasizing that it takes time just to internalize what is being learned in the *LifeKeys* class. Ask participants to think about how far they have progressed through

      identifying their gifts;

      knowing where they might put them to use;

      confidently seeking God's purposes.

   • While there are seasons of life that force us to be overly busy, God does not intend for us to be so busy that we lack time for what is truly important to Him and us.

   • Remind participants to be honest with themselves about what keeps them from getting to the things they have identified in *LifeKeys* as being of utmost value.

3. **Small group exercise** (30 minutes)

Break participants into four groups to discuss the first four biblical principles of time management, assigning a small group leader to each group. (State that the fifth principle, on using time for others, will be discussed at length in the final session.) Each person should join the group discussing the principle they believe they handle *best*.

Have each group record on overhead sheets or large flip-chart pages any hints or methods that proved beneficial to them as they have managed this area of their lives.

Allow twenty minutes for the groups to brainstorm together. Then gather again as a large group and allow a spokesperson from each of the four groups to share their insights. Encourage participants to record some of the suggestions for the areas where they have the greatest needs and make a commitment to try at least one or two of the ideas during the next month. We suggest collecting the lists to develop a handout of all of the practice suggestions. (One of these lists is shared on pages 215–217 as part of the exercise.)

4. **Closing** (20 minutes)

Refer people to LifeKeys Notations, page 239, and encourage participants to complete these pages before the final session. Allow for questions and emphasize that participants generally fall into three categories at this stage in the class:

- Some feel that they have much more self-discovery to do. They may be interested in retaking the class or working with someone one-on-one to complete what they have started. Some may just want to know more about resources available to them to continue this process.

- Others believe they have a much better understanding of themselves and want to learn about how they can apply this self-awareness to their current relationships and in their work, home, or volunteer settings.

- Others are ready to make a commitment to some new service opportunity or to make other changes, based upon their gifts and passions.

Reassure people that each stage is fine. Much depends on where they started.

Session 8—Service

We hope that *LifeKeys* has allowed participants to come to a new understanding of what the Bible means by "service" or "servant-hood." For many, this will be a breath of fresh air as they grasp the truth that fulfillment can come through the purposes God has chosen for them.

This session is designed to inspire participants to take their next step. Many of our participants wish that the class could meet a few more times. You may even want to schedule a follow-up reunion time as we have done occasionally.

Classtime Flow

1. **Small group time, questions** (15 minutes)

   - Allow participants time to complete LifeKeys Notations.

   - Inform people of several ways they can continue to process what they have learned. Many participants will want to sign up for some one-on-one counseling. Some may want to meet further with the leadership team, a previous *LifeKeys* graduate, a spiritual director, or volunteer coordinator. Outline how they might learn of available volunteer opportunities in your organization. Share what some others have done as a result of being in a *LifeKeys* seminar.

   - This is also a great time to get a list of possible volunteers for the next offering of a *LifeKeys* class.

2. **Lecture on service** (30 minutes)

   Review Chapter 8 to plan your lecture. Key points:

   - Serve from a place of fullness, not emptiness.

   - Biblical servants ensure that their own needs are met so they can focus on the needs of others.

   - Finding ways to use one's giftedness for God requires a conscious commitment. God leaves the choice of serving or not serving in people's hands.

- As we open our hearts to God's purposes, we become available to move to the places where God wants us to be.

- Following God's leading does not always lead to the world's approval. What will surely result is your own fulfillment as an instrument of God.

- The right place to serve is where God calls you to serve, whether far away or right where you are.

3. **Closing commitment service** (30 minutes)

As they finish this class, many participants will be ready to commit to a significant change in how they view who they are, why they're here, and what they do best. Finishing the *LifeKeys* class with a prayer and commitment service met the needs of our participants to confirm their desire to step out in faith and act on their commitments.

We suggest moving the class to a chapel or other worship environment for the commitment service. What follows is our format. Feel free to use our ideas, but your own creativity may produce a better idea.

- Share the list of expectations collected at the first session. Relate that many of these were high, broad, and complicated.

- Read *A Tale of Three Trees*[6] a folk tale about three trees who thought their dreams were crushed, only to discover that God had better plans for them. You could also read Chapter 9 aloud to set this same tone, or

- Show a film clip from *The Wizard of Oz* where the Wizard gives the Scarecrow his brains, the Tin Man his heart, and the Lion his courage. *The message affirms that the characters already had those things within them.*

- Give everyone a chance to fill out a "commitment slip" as described on pages 236–237. They need not put their names on this slip. What they write may be a commitment to a ser-

---

[6]Angela Elwell Hunt, *The Tale of Three Trees* (Batavia, Ill.: Lion Publishing, 1989).

vice opportunity or something that will help them better understand themselves or God. Some special music could be played during this time. Leave a few minutes of silence for those who need quiet to think.

- Have each small group come forward together and place their commitment slips in an offering basket.

- At this point, give each participant a certificate (we use different forms for men and women) that reads as follows:

The leaders for *LifeKeys*

Desire to officially confirm that

(participant's name)

Believing that he (she) is fearfully and

wonderfully made,

Has successfully begun the identification of his (her)

Life Gifts, Spiritual Gifts, Personality Type,

Values and Passions

Given by God for His Purposes

And hereby commits to move forward in faith

to do those good works which God has prepared in

advance specifically for each of us.

- Close with prayer.

SUGGESTIONS FOR FURTHER READING

Chapter 1

Bolles, Richard N. *What Color Is Your Parachute?* Berkeley: Ten Speed Press, 1996.

Brand, Dr. Paul, and Philip Yancey. *In His Image.* Grand Rapids, Mich.: Zondervan, 1984.

Chapter 2—Life Gifts

Bradley, John, and Jay Carty. *Discovering Your Natural Talents.* Colorado Springs: NavPress, 1994.

Hirsh and Kise. *Strong Interest Inventory™ Resource: Strategies for Group and Individual Interpretations in Business and Organizational Settings.* Palo Alto, Calif.: Consulting Psychologists Press, Inc. 1995.

Holland, John. *Making Vocational Choices.* Odessa, Fla.: Psychological Assessment Resources, Inc., 1992.

Chapter 3—Spiritual Gifts

Christopher, James A. *Gifts Believers Seek: The Work of the Holy Spirit in Mainstream Churches.* New York, N.Y.: The Pilgrim Press, 1988.

Swindoll, Charles R. *Flying Closer to the Flame.* Dallas: Word Publishing, 1993.

Chapter 4—Personality Types

Duncan, Bruce. *Pray Your Way: Your Personality and God.* London: Daron, Longman and Todd Ltd., 1993.

Harbaugh, Gary L. *God's Gifted People*. Minneapolis, Minn.: Augsburg Publishing House, 1988.

Hirsh, Sandra, and Jean Kummerow. *Introduction to Type in Organizations*, second edition. Palo Alto, Calif.: Consulting Psychologists Press, Inc., 1990.

Hirsh. *Using the Myers-Briggs Type Indictator in Organizations*, second edition. Palo Alto, Calif.: Consulting Psychologists Press, Inc., 1991.

Hirsh, with Jane Kise. *Work It Out: Clues to Solving People Problems at Work*. Palo Alto, Calif.: Davies-Black Publishing, 1996.

Michael, Chester P., and Norrisey, Marie C. *Prayer and Temperament: Different Prayer Forms for Different Personality Types*. Charlottesville, Va.: The Open Door, Inc., 1991

Oswald, Roy M., and Kroeger, Otto. *Personality Type and Religious Leadership*. Washington, D. C., The Alban Institute, 1988.

Chapter 5—Values

Covey, Stephen R. *The Seven Habits of Highly Effective People: Restoring the Character Ethic*. New York: Simon & Schuster, Fireside Edition, 1990.

Chapter 6—Passions

Seamands, David A. *Living With Your Dreams*. Wheaton, Ill.: Victor Books, 1990.

Chapter 7—Life Choices

Covey, Stephen R., A. Roger Merrill, and Rebecca R. Merrill. *First Things First*. New York, Simon & Schuster, 1994.

Foster, Richard J. *Celebration of Discipline, Revised Edition*. New York: Harper & Row, 1988.

Shedd, Charlie W. *Time for All Things*. Nashville: Abingdon Press, 1962.

Chapter 8—Service

Hansel, Tim. *Holy Sweat*. Dallas: Word Books, 1987.

Accuracy

Being true or correct in attention to detail

Achievement

Enjoying a sense of accomplishment

Advancement

Striving to move ahead rapidly, gaining opportunities for growth or seniority

Adventure

Seeking new and exciting challenges which may include taking risks

Aesthetics

Appreciating what is beautiful

Artistic Expression

Expressing self through the arts—painting, drama, literature, etc.

Authenticity

Ongoing desire to honestly express who one is

Balance

Giving proper weight to each area of a person's life

Challenge

Attracted to new problems, difficult tasks

Competency

Wanting to meet or exceed standards or expectations

Competition

Matching efforts or abilities with self or others

Conformity

Preferring to be like others, not standing out

Contribution

Giving or making a difference for others

Control

Being in charge or wanting to have influence over outcomes

Cooperation

Striving for congenial relationships and teamwork

Creativity

Being imaginative and innovative, going outside the norm

Efficiency

Working to accomplish tasks in comparatively little time

Fairness

Giving everyone an equal chance

Family

Placing importance on maintaining familial relationships

Financial Security

Being free from financial worries

Flexibility

Coping easily with change and surprise

Friendship

Placing importance on close, personal relationships

Generosity

Giving readily or liberally

Happiness

Finding satisfaction, joy, or pleasure

Humor

Enjoying the witty or amusing

Independence

Wanting control of own time, behavior, tasks

Influence

Capacity to affect or shape people, processes, or ideas

Integrity

Maintaining congruity between what one claims to be and how one acts

Learning

Lifelong commitment to growing in understanding

Leisure

Appreciating unstructured or unscheduled time

Location

Preferring a specific place, neighborhood, or area of country that matches lifestyle

Love

Cherishing oneself or others

Loyalty

Seeking to be faithful, constant, and steadfast

Nature

Finding joy and renewal in the out-of-doors

Organization

Being in control of time, priorities, possessions, and processes

Peace

Desiring tranquility, serenity, lack of discord

Perseverance

Sustaining momentum, having fortitude

Personal Development

Wanting to use one's potential and grow to the fullest

Physical Fitness & Health

Healthy regard for one's body, enjoying sports involvement

Power

Seeking to sell, persuade, lead, or influence others

Prestige

Having or showing success, rank, wealth, or status

Recognition

Desiring the respect of others or credit for achievements

Religious Beliefs

Sustaining faith in a higher power

Responsibility

Being accountable for outcomes

Security

Feeling safe and confident about the future

Self Respect

Having pride or a sense of personal identity

Service

Helping others or contributing to society

Stability

Maintaining continuity, consistency, and predictability over a period of time

Tolerance

Accepting or remaining open to the viewpoints and values of others

Tradition

Treasuring customs and links with the past

Variety

Desiring new and different
activities, frequent change

These are very valuable to me

These are valuable to me

These are not very valuable to me